How to Survive on
$50,000 to $150,000 a Year

BOOKS BY ROBERT WOOL

All You Need to Know About the IRS: A Taxpayer's Guide,
with Paul N. Strassels

All You Need to Know About Banks,
with John A. Cook

How to Survive on $50,000 to $150,000 a Year,
with Stanley J. Cohen

How to Survive on $50,000 to $150,000 a Year

Stanley J. Cohen
and Robert Wool

Houghton Mifflin Company *Boston* 1984

Contents

CHAPTER 1

W^{here} does it all go?

WHERE DOES it all go?

You're earning what you consider fairly big bucks — fifty, seventy-five, a hundred thousand dollars, more — but what have you got to show for it?

To be sure, you're living pretty well. You enjoy your apartment or house, though you could always use a bit more room, a slightly better location. And there's certainly no question about eating properly. Everything seems to get more and more expensive at the supermarket, never mind restaurants, but you and your family are eating well, and if you feel like it, there's a bottle of Bordeaux on the table too.

And though the same is true of clothes and prices, nobody in your house wears rags exactly.

But we are not concerned with poverty levels here. We're concerned with prosperity.

Ten, fifteen years ago, when you looked ahead you thought that if you ever earned $60,000, say, or $90,000 with two incomes in the family, you'd be rich. Yet here you are, you and your wife are pulling in $90,000, and one thing you're sure of: You're not rich. And you don't know why or what you can do about it.

People come to me for a financial plan, and they tell me that years ago they always figured that if they could earn $150,000 a year for three or four years straight, they'd retire. The game would be over and they'd have won. They sit in my office and tell me they've been making $150,000 or more for the last half-dozen years and they can't even see the light at the end of the tunnel.

As I say to them, no magic, no miracles. But have a bit of faith. There are countless steps we can take, plans and strategies we can devise, techniques and instruments we can apply that can change your financial life. We can not only solve the mystery of where it all goes, but cause it to go in whole new directions, ones that will allow you to accumulate some wealth for a change. For nearly twenty years as a financial planner and a stockbroker, that's what I've been doing for my clients and that's what I'll try to do with you through the course of this book.

When it comes to financial planning and managing your money, in fact, there is much that most people don't know because they are never exposed to it. That includes you and millions like you who might be earning very good livings, but handling or managing money is not central to your lives. An awful lot of my clients, for example, are doctors, dentists, lawyers, all well-educated professional people, good at what they do, some even famous, and they earn an easy $150,000 a year, often more. Money matters to them; they enjoy what it brings. But their grasp of the subject, at least when we start out, usually consists of misinformation about tax shelters and dreadful tips from relatives about buying real estate and/or "the next Xerox."

Ordering their financial conditions, however, is not so simple. They are about as well equipped to do that as I am to replace one of them and perform open-heart surgery or argue a case before the Supreme Court.

Interestingly, I have a number of other clients who are business men and women. They make and sell plastics and dresses and computer parts and furniture and other things, and their work obviously connects them quite directly with making money. As we'll see in Chapters 4 and 5, the financial vice-president of a chemical company in Texas managed his corporation's business affairs with great skill and sophistication; nonetheless the way he was running his own investments in the stock market, and his own personal money affairs, was disastrous.

Which is another way of saying that you might think of yourself as a financial illiterate, or as reasonably experienced when it comes to business and finance, yet still be shaking your head and rubbing your eyes, trying to figure out what is happening to your money, anxiously looking ahead and wondering if it is possible to stop this invisible yet steady erosion. The answer is, happily, by all means. As the wise man said, "It's easy if you know how."

First, perception.

You are not earning what you think you are earning. Or what you thought you would be earning if you reached this point when you looked up at it ten or fifteen years ago.

You are a vice-president of your company and they pay you $65,000 a year. Fifteen years ago, the man who had your job was paid $25,000. And if you think back, you'll recall that in those days $25,000 seemed like a lot of money. And it was.

The dollar was worth more, bought more in those days. Inflation was less in those days. A big dinner for two back then cost you about $30; you're lucky to do it today for less than $75 to $100. You bought a house for $40,000 in 1968. Today you can sell it for $170,000. A Chevrolet, a plain old working man's Chevrolet, these days will cost you $10,000.

You know the litany: What a loaf of bread used to cost compared with today, or a ticket to the movies, even a lousy hot dog at the ballgame. Four times a year all those figures get tossed at you on your nightly TV news program as a feeble way of explaining why you're frustrated.

But in a sense such numbers miss the point. You've got

to adjust the way you think of your supposed big bucks. You must stop looking at your earnings as if you were pulling down $75,000 or $80,000 and it were still 1965 or 1970 or earlier. You don't have the buying power you would have had in those days.

It may violate your sense of accomplishment — which could also be inflated — but for a sense of reality, you're better off thinking of your $75,000 or $80,000 as if it were more like $30,000 or $40,000 in old-fashioned dollars. Or to bring it a bit more up-to-date, in 1983 you needed an income of $60,000 to match an income of $40,000 in 1977.

Alas, it's a little like having a big title but not that much power.

Inflation and taxes, inflation and taxes, inflation and taxes

Even though you are absolutely the best vice-president your company ever had and a wonderful human being, inflation, among other things, has inflated your salary to figures that still sound impressive but in truth are not.

Inflation affects all my thinking when I develop financial plans. While I find most people overlook it, to me it's as real as taxes — another element of life people tend to overlook when it comes to their finances.

A widow came to me for a plan, reluctantly, she told me. All her closest friends had badgered her into it. She didn't see why she needed me, because her husband, who had died two years ago, had left her nearly $500,000 and a mortgage-free home. Their two children were almost on their own, one finishing college with a promising job in hand, the other with a year left of law school. Being very conservative, she had taken all the money left to her and divided it among certificates of deposit (CDs) at her bank, a money market fund and a high-interest savings account. She figured that she was averaging about a 9% return on her money, and most importantly, it was all safe.

Beyond that income, she earned $48,000 from her job with an advertising agency, which meant that she had something more than $90,000 a year, she told me, which was more than enough.

In my line of work, I sigh a lot, as you'll see. It was true, I told her, that she had security, but she also had a guaranteed loss. "If the bank pays you 9% a year, you're losing money. A federally insured guaranteed loss," I said as gently as I could.

She stared at me with absolute hostility and fear.

"Really, Mrs. Connell. I'm not trying to scare you. But look at the arithmetic. You're talking 9% before taxes and before inflation," I explained. "You are now filing as a single person, and without looking at your tax returns, I can tell you you're going to be in the 50% tax bracket. Not everything you earn will be taxed at the 50% rate, but part of it will be. We have to look at the interest income as if it were piled on top of your salary from your job, and part of it falls into your highest bracket, some into the 48% bracket. Which means that you start with a 9% return on your money, and when you finish with federal taxes, you're down to 4½%. You live in Connecticut, where there are no personal income taxes, so we don't have to take anything more out for state taxes. But still, when we factor in inflation, which currently is running about 6%, I have bad news for you, Mrs. Connell. That money you have loaned to the bank and for which they are paying you a guaranteed 9% and which a few minutes ago looked very nice to you is really a certified loss on your money."

Mrs. Connell refused to believe me at first, like other clients in similar situations, and I had to run through the numbers several times with her.

Finally it all registered. Even then she didn't want to jump into any real financial plan immediately. Her fears of risk were so great that she had to wait and think about it, call me several times over the ensuing months before she could actually bring herself to make some fairly modest different investments with her money.

But Mrs. Connell is not uncommon. Think about your own investments. Think about the times you've had a stock go up 15%. You took your money and ran. You celebrated. But suppose you had owned that stock for less than a year and a day. Then you had a "short-term capital gain," and you'd be taxed on your profit as if it were "ordinary income" — at the highest levels.

Which means you've earned only 7.5% on your hot tip if you're in the 50% bracket, and if you live in New York City, as I do, that amount shrinks to 6.19% when you figure state and local taxes. On top of which there is that inflation figure. With inflation you are probably losing money on that glowing 15% return.

But as we'll see, life need not play such dirty and cruel tricks on you.

Maybe you could have let that stock ride until you had owned it for a year and a day. Then you would have got yourself a "long-term capital gain," on which you would have 60% of your gain tax-free. In your bracket, that means you would be paying the Feds only 20% on your gain (which is your 50% rate times the taxable 40% of your gain).

Or maybe you might have let that stock run for a much longer time if your approach to picking stocks and reading the market were different, as we'll see in Chapters 10 and 11. Maybe then instead of a 15% return, we're talking about a 50% or 150% return.

Or maybe you shouldn't have bought that stock at all, no matter how promising the tip was. Maybe, considering your whole financial profile, what you should have done with that $5000 was invest it in a tax-exempt bond trust or in a public utility stock with a tax-advantaged dividend reinvestment plan (Chapter 12), or maybe put it into an aggressive mutual fund, which can be a great generator of long-term capital gains (Chapter 4) or any number of things that are tax-smart.

Being tax-smart is at the heart of all my planning. It has to be. Almost all my clients are in the 50% bracket. Whenever I recommend a move to them, I must always consider the tax consequences first, and that's the way you should also begin to look at your earnings and all your finances: What is the tax effect going to be?

Where does all your salary go? Well, unless you take full advantage of the law and start to make some intelligent and sophisticated moves, unless you have a real, balanced financial plan, you're going to be handing a huge chunk of your salary to the Feds.

You've hit the once-magical gorgeously round number of $100,000 a year? Well, once Melvin your accountant finishes playing around with your return, maybe he's got you deducted down to, say, $85,600. That's your net taxable income. For 1983, you'd pay the Feds $27,278 on that basis, which would leave you $58,322 and one answer to your question, "Where does it all go?"

But it need not be that way. The law does not require you to be so generous to your federal government, or any local ones either. You can still be a terrific citizen and keep more of your own money, but to do it you have to start by looking at taxes in a whole new way. That business of perception again.

Taxes are more than that annual painful bother, that dreadful afternoon you spend with Melvin once a year near the end of March, when you pass him all of your American Express and Visa receipts and canceled checks for what you maintain with a straight face are business expenses, and have your annual tug-of-war with him about combined business-vacation trips and deductions you piously declare you are entitled to, and which he shrinks away from, feeling the omnipresent hot breath of the IRS on his neck.

Taxes are much more than that. In your bracket they must become an integral part of any investment move you even think about, as real a number as the projected return you read about in a prospectus.

Point is, as we'll see, there are plenty of possibilities, bright possibilities and tax-smart uses for your money that are all geared to earning you more and letting you keep it, despite taxes and inflation.

There really is hope.

A few words on tax brackets and onions

Who is in the charmed 50% bracket? The tax law was changed in 1981, and according to that, for 1983 earnings you'll qualify if you show taxable income — not gross earnings, but net taxable income — of $55,300 if you're single, $109,400 if you file jointly.

After 1983, those levels will rise to $81,800 for single people and $162,400 for couples. Which seems like a lot, but before you cheer, let me tell you that you'll be in a 49% bracket if you show anything between $55,300 and $81,800 as a single or $109,400 and $162,400 for you and your spouse. And if you two have as much as $85,600, which is a bit more than half the 50% level, you'll still be in the 45% bracket.

Also, never forget state and local taxes. If you're close to the 50% bracket, when you add those on (as most people must), they'll push you over the mark.

And there's always inflation boosting your earnings and so boosting you into higher brackets.

As you learned back in Economics 101, this does not mean that 49% or 50% of every penny you earn is going to be taken away. As you also learned then, we have this wondrous graduated federal income tax, which starts out at zero and gets progressively higher until it reaches the 50% bracket, when in fact 50% of every dollar you earn over that amount will be taken away by the IRS.

If you're like most of my clients, your Economics 101 course was not all that good to begin with, and whatever you did learn about taxes has faded with the years.

I recommend the onion. Visualize an onion, I tell them, with layers upon layers. What you see is a tax onion. (I know that's juvenile and corny, but I'll do almost anything to make this clear. I even used to tell clients that a tax onion is sure to make them cry, but I stopped because I never got the kind of laughs I expected with that one.)

At the onion's core, in 1984, is the zero tax bracket, $3400. The first $3400 of income that you and your spouse have is tax-free. All the money from $3400 to $5500 is the next layer of the onion; it's taxed at the rate of 11%. All the money you show from $5500 to $7600, at the rate of 12%. All the money from $7600 to $11,900 at 14%. And so on, layer after layer, bracket after bracket. As you go higher, the brackets widen, so where we had a range of $4300 for the 14% bracket, we have a spread of $53,000 reaching from 49% to 50%.

The IRS adds up your onion layers. They take the amount of taxable income you show in each bracket, multiply it by the tax rate for that bracket — 11%, 12% and so on — and charge you the total of all those amounts. That's the effect of the computation you see in the tax table that comes with your return.

So, Mr. Wonderful in the golden $100,000 circle, we saw your deductions take you down to $85,600, on which you paid the IRS $27,278. That means you paid them 32% of your taxable income, and that is your "average tax rate." Your "marginal tax bracket," however, is 48%. Every additional penny you earn will be taxed at the rate of 48% and will rise to 50%, the maximum the law now allows.

What is terribly important about all this when it comes

to planning is that any investment income you earn will be taxed at your marginal rate — your highest rate.

And that is why I ruined your celebration party when you had just walked away with a 15% gain on a hot stock tip.

And that is why you can't make an investment or financial-planning move without thinking about the tax bite.

Would you like to be a millionaire?

Simple.

Take $10,000, invest it in anything that returns you 8% a year, don't touch any of the earnings, allow the earnings to compound and wait sixty years. In sixty years your $10,000 will have compounded to $1 million.

If you don't think you'll be around in sixty years to enjoy your wealth, do it for your five-year-old child. It will save him or her the trouble of having to create a retirement plan (providing, of course, that we don't have 8% inflation, in which case the $1 million will have exactly the purchasing power of $10,000).

Such are the joys of compounding, which has been pronounced "the eighth wonder of the world."

It's a wonder that I try to turn to my advantage wherever I can and whenever possible, without paying taxes for now at least.

As we'll see, there are several investment strategies in which we increase our assets enormously by letting our investments compound for a number of years.

It's one way that you can painlessly pull together enough money, say $85,000, to pay for four years of college when your kid starts at Cornell in eight years (Chapter 15).

Or it's a way to build your retirement fund, whether it's one from your corporation or an IRA or Keogh. You make regular investments year after year, the earnings compound year after year and the tax law allows you to defer taxes on retirement-fund earnings until you start withdrawing the money. That's how your modest $2000 yearly contribution to your IRA can become more than $80,000 in ten years. (All of this in Chapter 16, "Planning for retirement.")

We find compounding in tax-exempt bond funds. All the interest is tax-exempt, of course, and if you let it stay in the fund and be reinvested, over twenty years it can make the difference between your having a portfolio worth $200,000 and one worth $600,000 (Chapter 12).

Or we can use compounding with single-premium deferred annuities, a low-risk instrument that allows your investment to balloon over the years for retirement purposes or any other.

Now, I don't pretend that compounding your money is an especially sophisticated matter. But it is often an overlooked element that makes a vast difference in the whole effort to build your assets. Once you begin to see how it can work in your own financial life, you possess one new perspective. And new perspectives are very much what I'm reaching for in this book.

Building assets

Earlier I spoke of an invisible erosion of your earnings. By the end of this book, you'll have a kit full of techniques to end that slow, implacable seepage.

I hope that's only the beginning. That's the least you must do to survive. Beyond that, we'll examine a number of ways you can start to prosper. "Building assets," it's called — a chunky term, but one that has a certain poetry about it once you get to know what it really means.

I've already begun to suggest some of the maneuvers we'll consider. We'll also spend a fair amount of time looking at the stock market, at how to buy stocks, how to know when to sell them, how to let your profits run and cut your losses, in the cliché of Wall Street.

The stock market is the primary place, in my view, to build your assets. There are other ways and places, such as real estate, which we'll also consider, but as a planner the market comes first.

If you're like an awful lot of people who come to me, you've invested in the market or, more accurately, played the market for one of two reasons, maybe even both in combination: (1) You got a tip from a friend, relative or colleague who talks frequently and loudly of his killings in the market. Needless to say, the tip is both "hot" and "can't miss." (2) You got sold on it by a broker who sounds as if he really knows what he's talking about, quoting you "P/E ratios," practically whispering into the phone about a company's newest miracle product that is going to be announced any day now. In a quinella, you not only are being hustled by a broker, he also is acting on a tip.

I have news for you. There really are more rational ways to invest in the market. There are various approaches that give you a chance to evaluate the company whose stock you're considering, to look at that company in relation to others in its group as well as to the market at large. There are ways you can examine the stock's history, just as you can read the history and patterns of the whole market, both of which can be critical in determining the optimum time for buying a stock or selling it.

In Chapters 10 and 11, I spread out the methods I use. They are not the only ones in creation, but they certainly have been successful for me. You might use them, adapt them, chew them apart with your broker.

In fact, there are aspects of them I point out that are probably beyond your reach right now, take more time than you have, require more information than you have access to. Still, I want to share them with you for a variety of reasons.

First, because I know that a vast number of people do invest their money in the market for no sensible reasons, and if you're one of them, I'd like to stop you. Whether you decide to follow my technique or not, I hope that after you read what I do, you'll never be able to toss your money into the market on a pure gamble again. That you'll never be able to listen to your hotshot friend or broker the same way again.

In fact, in a larger sense that's what I hope to do with this book: affect you so you can never look at your financial life the same way again.

I try to do it with my clients during the hours and sessions we sit evolving their financial plans.

I guess the transcendent objective is to give them and you enough knowledge so that you can begin to gain control over your own financial life. End this angst that mysterious demons are mauling you and all your hard-earned riches, demons you can't see or exorcise. End the helpless feeling that there is no way you can survive, never mind prosper.

Now let us scheme together.

CHAPTER 2

What I look for and you should too

GETTING CONTROL is what it's all about.

The pieces seem to be all over the place. People come to me knowing that something is certainly wrong with the way their financial lives are going. But they can't figure out where that great leak is or how to plug it.

Usually I start by sorting out what they have, what's coming in and what's going out. What are you doing with your money? I ask. An obvious but not simple question. Once the sorting out is done, and it's usually the first time it's ever been done, then we can begin to look at where they want to go and, being realistic, to see if we can devise some plans to get there.

To get our basic information, there are thirteen different aspects of people's lives I explore with them. And it really is an exploration. Few people have actually unearthed this essential stuff before.

Ask yourself the question, What am I doing with my money? Specifically? To the dollar?

The answers are not all in your head. They are in your checkbooks, your canceled checks, your records, such as they are. Maybe at your accountant's office or in your lawyer's files. Pulling it all together is a project that often takes weeks.

To smooth the process, I ask the questions that follow in this chapter. Let's consider them first, and then in the next chapter we can examine some interesting patterns that frequently emerge from this probing. Several of these areas we'll cover in detail later in the book.

1. *What's your net worth?* What do you now earn, what have you earned for the last three years? What do you own? Home? Stocks, bonds, other investments? Property? Valuable paintings, silver, household possessions? Checking accounts, savings accounts? Life insurance?

Here we're doing a couple of things. First, I'm trying to get a real idea of what you are worth and give you, at last, a clear picture as well. For most people the bottom line is surprisingly higher than they imagined.

Further, in sorting out your assets we're going to get our first overview of your investments and see what kind of balance they reflect.

Frequently I find the largest asset you have is your home, and frequently people object to my including it in their net-worth total. "That's play money," they tell me. "I'm not going to sell my house. So what if it's worth $225,000 on the market? I can't get my hands on that money."

But they're wrong. First of all, when we consider net worth, in part we're considering overall financial security. Looked at that way, a man might die, his wife might sell that house and move to something smaller, and the value of that house certainly will matter to her.

Also, when people tell me that the market value doesn't matter in the real world, I often ask them if their house has been appreciating in recent years. Sure, they reply, and we figure that it has been getting more valuable at about, say, 12% a year.

That's $12,000 a year on a house worth $100,000. We're talking $24,000 on a $200,000 house.

Looked at that way, clients begin to gain a new perspective on their homes, and I find it also helps them to think about their financial goals differently.

Further, as we'll see in Chapter 8, you most definitely can get your hands on the money in your house. You can refinance your home.

As we examine the investments you now have, we want to do more than add up their value to give us a number for your net worth. We want to see if the investments are varied and balanced. Do you show nothing but fixed-income securities, no common stocks at all? Why so overloaded?

With variety and balance, if changes occur no one investment can sink you. Greater balance means greater security, but I rarely find sufficient balance when I look at the investments most people bring to me. They invest on the advice of stockbrokers, and even if a broker's research is good, his market sense astute, and he isn't merely after a quick commission, he still isn't looking at the whole condition. He's not planning for you. He's buying and selling for you.

2. *What does it cost you to live now?* Budgets are boring, but some analysis is necessary. When you fill in the blanks below, you can see where your money goes and you can see what sticks out. People continually surprise themselves at the amounts they spend each year for vacations, for recreation and entertainment.

I'm not a social worker and I don't try to change the way people live. If there is some ridiculously great expense, such as $100 a month for dry cleaners, I point it out. Usually, if I touch on some pleasurable item, say entertainment, I'm touching a sensitive spot. "That's the way we live," I'm told. "What's the point in working so hard if you can't enjoy what you earn?"

I don't argue with that. I take their reality and try to plan around it.

Pulling the data together for this review takes a bit of time, but it's well spent. The overview is essential. Here's what I ask for.

Food	$_____
Clothing	$_____
Housing (mortgage/rent)	$_____
Household repairs/maintenance/utilities	$_____
Household furnishings	$_____
Debt repayment (installment)	$_____
Property taxes	$_____
Property and liability insurance	$_____
Income taxes, social security taxes and so on	$_____
Transportation (auto, commuting)	$_____
Life insurance	$_____
Medical/dental (include insurance cost)	$_____
Vacations	$_____
Recreation and entertainment	$_____
Contributions/gifts	$_____
Education	$_____
Savings	$_____
Other	$_____
Total annual expenditures	$_____

3. *When it comes to investment, how much risk can you live with comfortably?* Are you most concerned with capital appreciation or capital preservation? Does the stock market make you nervous?

I've got to understand where you are in the spectrum of risk before I can create a plan that you're comfortable with. And risk is something most people don't give much thought to until pressed.

Often I find this attitude is based on the experience of parents. Anyone in his fifties knows what the Depression was. "My father was in real estate and he was foreclosed in '32. I don't want anything to do with real estate."

Perhaps a parent lost heavily in the stock market. Or, "I was left $200,000 in bonds, but they're only worth $110,000 today, so I certainly don't want anything to do with long-term bonds."

I can't change such deeply rooted feelings. But I make clear to such people that there is no such thing as a risk-free investment. In fact, where you have absolute certainty, you have an absolutely guaranteed loss, as we saw with Widow Connell in Chapter 1. If you put your money in the bank for an absolutely guaranteed rate of return, when you figure what inflation will be while the money is sitting there and what your taxes will be on the interest you earn, you'll find that you've given yourself an absolutely guaranteed loss. Your money will simply erode.

If you expect your assets to grow, which means that they will increase at a higher rate than inflation and taxes can diminish them, you must be prepared to accept some risk.

How much depends in part on your "risk quotient" and your particular situation.

If you're showing me nothing more than a net worth of $100,000 and you've got a good, secure job, reasonable insurance, then I'll tell you that we have to go in one direction and one direction only — we have to invest in stocks, and aggressively.

But if you're showing the same $100,000 net worth and things are shaky where you work, we might have to protect what you've got. Maybe all we can do for now is Treasury bills.

Years ago a friend of mine, Al Meisel, put $250,000, virtually all the money he had for investing, into high-quality tax-exempt bonds at 6%. He thought he had locked his money away safely and wisely, and I remember he tried to convince his brother Dick to do the same. Dick did buy a few tax-exempts, but he put money into growth stocks and real estate as well. The time came when interest rates soared and Al saw his tax-exempts drop in market value to $140,000; by then inflation made the $15,000 income they threw off look pretty small. Brother Dick, meanwhile, also lost on his tax-exempts, but he more than made up for those losses in profits and income from his stocks and real estate.

Safety comes from balance and proportion, not from blind faith in what you think is the most conservative investment.

To get specific with my clients, I ask them which of the following kinds of investments they've had experience with in the past, which make them very nervous, which they can live with and which don't worry them at all:

> Savings account
> Tax-incentive investments
> Government bonds
> Mutual funds
> Common stocks
> Municipal bonds
> Annuities
> Real estate
> Certificates of deposit
> Preferred stocks
> Corporate bonds

4. *What are you most concerned about right now?* Protection against inflation? Your current income? Keeping your money and assets "liquid," that is, in forms you can convert to cash quickly? Deferral of income taxes? Preserving what you've got? Making it grow? Income that you'll have in the future?

I get a sense of what people want during the course of an interview or two. It sort of comes out through suggestion rather than directly.

Often I find their vision of what might be done with their money altered by the success of a friend or relative in the market. A brother bought Polaroid and Xerox years and years ago and made a fortune. It would be nice if I could do the same thing, he says. It would be, I tell him, but you can't make a fortune today in Polaroid and Xerox.

I also find that people's vision is clouded by where they've been and the struggle they've had up to now. With one such couple I spent hours reviewing all their tax returns, going through everything we're discussing in this chapter, and then did a full plan for them. We met again after that and I showed them how we could cut their taxes, expand their investment portfolio, increase their assets considerably and arrange for them to retire comfortably.

The man nodded, even smiled a bit. His wife only shook her head.

"What's wrong?" I asked her.

She sighed. "Deep in my heart, I know we'll always be poor."

5. *What taxes do you pay?* Interestingly, an awful lot of people can't come close to telling me what they've actually paid. If they have substantial withholding from their paychecks, they never get the real figure in mind.

In a first reading of the returns, there are three important numbers I'm after. I want to see the total amount of dollars coming in from all sources. I want to check your net taxable income, the amount left after all deductions have been taken. And I want to see how much you've paid in taxes.

As I scan these returns, I'm beginning to shape the financial plan. Taxes are at the heart of any plan. I want to be sure you've taken advantage of all the deductions allowed on Schedule A. I want to see how much unearned taxable income you have, how much interest and dividend income. I want to check what you have in long-term capital gains.

6. *What are your goals and plans for your children?* So often these are taken for granted and never articulated in a way that we can put a price on them. Practically all of the

people who come to me intend to send their children to college, and in a general way they all know how expensive that can be. Hardly any of them, however, have a specific idea of what the cost is going to be in, say, ten years; even less, how they're going to pay it.

"My son is going to be some kind of professional, so I have three or four years beyond college," I'm told. Or, "My daughter will get at least a master's."

But are we talking about Harvard or a state school? There's a huge difference in cost. Is it likely the son or daughter will live at home and commute to college?

Once I get the answers to those questions, I can extrapolate and come up with some figures. If we are talking about an Ivy League school ten years from now, we take the $11,000 bill of today and factor inflation into our arithmetic. Obviously there is some guessing required here, but I estimate an inflation rate of 7% for the coming ten years.

We are then looking at a yearly cost of $21,600, which leaves my clients stunned and gasping. "Does that mean my kid can't go to college?" they ask.

It does not. As we'll see in Chapter 15, it means an investment plan that's going to create a college fund, it means "gifting" to the child year by year, taking advantage of every possible tax allowance, possibly establishing a Clifford trust.

7. *What happens if you die?* Or become disabled and can't work? What coverage do you have, if any, and what should you have?

There is often great confusion here. People working for large companies usually have group life insurance plans as benefits. Professionals, self-employed people, and associates in small corporations have a tougher time when it comes to insurance.

Often they have no disability insurance, I find, even though all of their income flow might stop if they are laid up for several months. But frequently they can buy cheap group insurance through their national associations or professional organizations.

Most people have no clear idea of what they really need. They might be carrying a large life insurance policy simply because someone sold it to them.

I am a licensed insurance broker. In Chapter 14 we'll discuss in detail how we can use insurance as part of your whole financial plan. A couple of observations now.

With a few exceptions, I don't believe in whole life insurance. Term insurance is cheaper, gives you the coverage you need for as long as you need it.

Only insure those people whose loss will matter to you financially. Why insure your young child? If he or she dies, the emotional loss will be incalculable, but there is no financial loss.

Still, I find that personal attitude matters greatly when it comes to insurance. I've had a number of clients with huge amounts of life insurance. When I sketch out a full plan for them, I show them how they can adequately protect their families with less insurance, building assets in other areas. They nod and say, "I still want it."

At any rate, seeing what is already there and, more importantly, what coverage is missing is enlightening and revealing to most of my clients. It's also something we can act on quite quickly.

8. *Do you have a will? A trust?* I encounter remarkable surprises with this item. People with substantial wealth often have no wills. Sometimes they tell me they meant to write a will, but it got so difficult deciding who would get what that they simply put it off.

Of course, without a will, I quickly point out, they are exposing their heirs to tremendous legal problems. Without a will they could end up with their home states determining how much goes to their wives and their children, and it could be a distortion of their own wishes.

I also find many people with outdated wills. As noted, the tax laws of 1981 and 1982 have substantially changed estate taxes and offer a number of new benefits. But you don't get them automatically. Your will must reflect awareness of the changes, and a will drawn in 1970 won't.

If I find wealth and no trusts, that's something I note and realize that we will have to consider carefully with a client's lawyer as we get into the big plan.

9. *What are your retirement plans?* How many years before you retire? What benefit plans do you now have — a pension plan, Keogh, IRA, deferred compensation? How much money a week, a year, do you think you'll need to live the way you want to when you retire?

Many people, young and middle-aged, give no thought to retirement at all. That seems so far in the future, they can't conceive of it right now. Or they're working so well, the idea of ever stopping or even cutting back is beyond them.

A doctor tells me that when he reaches seventy he'll give up his full-time practice, but he'll still be teaching or doing work at the hospital, possibly taking in a younger doctor as a partner. Or the businessman is simply going to keep on working, he thinks. Maybe he'll also teach a bit.

Not that there's anything wrong with their intentions, but the way such plans are presented to me is a way of saying, "Well, I really don't have to worry, I'll always be working and there'll always be money coming in, even if it's less than now."

Individual entrepreneurs often can't phase themselves out of their businesses. Without them there is no business. Sometimes they can sell their companies, staying on as consultants for, say, five years and bringing in some income that way.

Accountants often partially retire, working the tax season from January through April 15.

I try to press people to be specific and realistic. It's nice to think about teaching, but do you have anything firm to go on, contact with a college? And what happens if you can't sell the business and you can't find some suitable work as a consultant?

No matter what notions of retirement you might have, multiple retirement plans are essential. What are you and your wife doing with the retirement plans where you work, with plans offered through your union or professional association, with IRAs and Keoghs? Is there any way you can have part of your present salary deferred until you retire? Is a portion of your investment portfolio sufficiently long term so that it doesn't mature until you've retired, and your taxes on it are then also deferred until you've retired? When you stop working and your income drops dramatically, your taxes will too. That's when you want to have all of this deferred income finally coming due to you, a time when you'll need it to replace your previous regular earnings and a time when you'll pay much lower taxes on it.

You can't have too many retirement plans. Between my wife and me, we have nine. Every couple should have at least six.

How much are you going to need to live comfortably when you retire? A tough question because, again, we have to look years ahead and consider inflation.

Presumably your living expenses will decrease greatly. You'll save on everything connected to business, from commuting tickets to lunches and clothes. A client recently told me that he and his family spent $70,000 a year in aftertax dollars. But he thought they could live comfortably in retirement on about half of that, or $35,000. He was then fifty-five, planning to retire in ten years, and thought he'd have little trouble generating $35,000.

He was quite surprised when I factored in ten years of inflation at 7%, which meant that he'd have to show about $69,000 to yield the equivalent of $35,000 today.

But I didn't leave him trembling. As I showed him and as I'll show you in Chapter 16, there are a number of investment plans that, when combined with available retirement plans, can make a comfortable retirement possible.

10. *Do you expect to inherit anything?* Obviously, this information can be important for any plan I develop. But this is a very touchy area. People don't like to talk about it, as if they're dancing on someone's grave before the poor soul is even buried. They can't bring themselves to say, "Well, my mother is seventy-eight years old and her health really isn't so good. When she dies I will inherit about X thousand dollars."

Another difficult aspect of this concerns the aging mother or father. Changes in the tax law in 1981 allow a person to will great amounts of an estate tax-free to a relative other than a spouse. The law started with a $250,000 ceiling in 1981 and it will rise to $600,000 tax-free by 1987.

Which is good as far as it goes. Because $600,000 is a substantial amount, but not so large as it seems. Think for a moment about inflation and what has happened to the real estate market in recent years: Is a home worth $200,000 or $300,000 so uncommon these days? With that, you are a good way toward an estate of $600,000.

My point with clients is that there might well be something over $600,000 in that estate, and it will be taxed unless certain measures are taken. If, for example, the aging parent begins to make gifts to his or her children, the amount of unprotected value in the estate can be cut greatly, maybe wiped out altogether.

The problem comes when nobody wants to tell Mother or Dad to face the fact that he or she isn't going to live that

much longer. And nobody wants to tell parents to start giving away their money to their children. "You tell them,"
clients say to me. "If you do it, it'll be a professional, busi-
nesslike affair." I try not to. The aging parents resent me,
think I'm giving them advice I have no business offering or,
worse, imagine that their own children are plotting with me.

Not long ago my client, a lawyer, drew up all the papers
for his father's estate. The old man died and the estate had
to pay nearly $150,000 in taxes. The family was outraged. A
cousin, also a lawyer, told all the other cousins, brothers,
sisters, everyone in the will, that my client had been absolutely negligent. If my client had been any kind of lawyer,
he would have anticipated the tax burden and gotten the
money out of his father's hands. In fact, that's exactly what
my client tried to do. But every time he raised the matter
with his father, and it was always painful for him to do so,
the old man dismissed him. "You take care of my papers,"
he told his son. "I'll take care of my money."

11. *What's your present business?* What is its tax form,
that is, corporation, partnership, Subchapter S? What are your
plans for your share of it after you die?

All this information will become important as we develop
the plan. Though I don't advise clients on their businesses,
I do find that asking the questions above often causes them
to reexamine the legal and tax aspects of their organizations.

12. *Besides your spouse and children, do you have any
other dependents?* Who are they and what do you spend on
them? Are you planning to leave money to any person or
organization outside your immediate family? Is that in your
will?

This question relates to other areas, to current expenses
and to a complete will. Occasionally we get into some tax
maneuvering with charities. Mostly these questions are re-
minders.

13. *Above all, what do you want your financial plan to do for you?* When I talk with clients about this, I find a bit of overlap with the earlier question, the consideration of their greatest financial concerns.

By and large, people talk about getting on top of their financial affairs, getting a grasp, not letting so much happen by accident. They want to apply techniques they have heard about, even if they don't fully understand them. They want to keep more of the money they earn and see it grow.

I make the point with them that we should try for a holistic approach to their affairs so that we can pull all the ends together and organize their whole financial life. They have their dreams and hopes, and we should consider them and see if we can create a plan that puts those dreams and hopes through a calculator and makes them real.

CHAPTER 3

What I usually find

To UNDERSTAND clients, obviously I need data. But I also have to get a feel for their attitudes, their hopes. What changes do they have in mind for their financial lives, and how do they think those lives can be reshaped? Are their visions realistic? How do they look at money?

In two lengthy sessions with them, perhaps a couple of hours each, mostly I let them talk. Frequently we'll gather over dinner, which is less constricting than meeting in an office, and we can relax and let the conversation flow. If the planning is for a couple, which is usually the case, it's important for me that both are there. I don't want to create a plan for a man and have it disturb his wife.

Many financial planners use elaborate questionnaires, which they analyze and dissect by computer, printing out 150 pages or more. At one time I worked that way, but I found the plans got too mechanical. Now I prefer the meetings, scribbling my own notes, keeping others in my head and custom-fitting each plan out of all that.

I supplement this with the two tables mentioned in the previous chapter: their budget, which shows me how they spend their money now, and that simple risk/stress chart, which gives me a feel for their tolerance for risk when it comes to investments.

At times this process gets spread over several weeks. Sometimes at the first meeting, the material we unearth and examine disturbs people sufficiently that everything gets delayed. They have considerable difficulty, for example, figuring out what they actually spend or gathering the other information I need, such as facts on their retirement plans.

But by the time we have gone through all this, I have a plan pretty well sketched out in my mind, if not on paper, and I also have a very clear idea of the client's greatest areas of confusion and ignorance.

Let me mention some of the most common ones. They may be familiar to you.

Investing in tax-smart ways. It's not enough to pick a good stock, invest and make a profit, even though a vast number of people think that's what investing is all about.

So far as I'm concerned, the only smart investment for anyone in a high tax bracket is one in which your profits are tax-free or tax-deferred or that has some other tax advantages.

In the next two chapters, we'll look at the problems one of my Texas clients had. The man loves to play the market, was picking good stocks and averaging a profit of 20% on his money, which he and millions like him would consider a very nice return. But that is because he and millions like him ignore the effect of taxes on their sweet 20% profit.

Thinking tax-smart when it comes to investments is critical. In these and other chapters, we'll examine several strategies and the instruments to use: tax-exempt bonds and bond trusts; public utilities; long-term capital gains and how you might use mutual funds to build them; real estate, and oil and gas shelters.

Custodial accounts. A divorced woman comes to me showing an annual income of $125,000 a year. Her eleven-year-old son lives with her in the co-op she owns. The stock market makes her very nervous, she says, so she has $75,000 in a money market fund, at the time earning her about 10%.

One of the things I point out to her is that whatever she earns in that fund, it's going to be taxed as regular income. Under her existing situation— which could change greatly to her advantage — that means handing half her interest income to the federal government.

However, the tax law offers her a nice alternative. It allows her to take $10,000 a year and give it to her son as a gift, and she does not have to pay any gift tax.

"Can I take a deduction for that amount?" she asks.

"No, but you'll save taxes in another way."

I explain that the $10,000 could then be invested in her son's name. The money would belong to him, but she would control it. She would be the "custodian." Then whatever the money earns would be taxed only at his level, not hers. Since the boy has no other earnings, the amount he'd have to pay might be zero or close to it. If the money went into the same money market fund, earned the same 10%, and that was all the kid earned that year, he'd file a tax return showing $1000. That first thousand would be tax-free. If there were another thousand, it would be taxed at 14%.

Not only a simple way to cut the taxes she would otherwise pay, but a good way to start building a fund for the boy. And if he wanted to, the tax law allows her ex-husband to make an additional $10,000 gift to the boy.

Think about that. The law allows gifts of $10,000 a year from each parent to each child. Think about the amount of money you can shift out of your own taxable pile while creating a substantial controllable fund for your child over the years, with low, low taxes on its earnings.

The limitations of accountants. A couple came to me, jointly earning about $140,000 a year. Nancy was a very successful advertising executive; Eric published newsletters, owned his own company. They were somewhat shell-shocked by the time they reached me. Shortly before, they had paid some $55,000 in federal income taxes, scrambling to put together about $25,000 cash to cover the taxes that had not been withheld.

When their accountant called them with the chilling results of his calculations, he did not seem surprised or chagrined. These were the numbers, period. Although not sadistic, they told me, his attitude seemed fatalistic: You've made a lot of money, so you should expect to pay a lot of taxes.

After the shock and the scrambling, Eric reviewed their returns for that painful year, as well as those for the previous two years, which had been prepared by the same accountant. Although their taxes had been lower in previous years and there had been less cash to raise over the amount withheld, one year they had to pay an additional $26,000, the other about $30,000. He called the accountant. "How can this happen?" he asked. "I don't know much about this, but isn't there some way we can shelter some of our income or do something so that we don't pay so much in taxes? I mean, we both earn well, but people who make us look like paupers don't pay any taxes at all."

"Gee," the accountant replied, "I have clients who make much more than you and Nancy, and they don't shelter anything."

"What do they do?"

"They pay more taxes, but they sleep at night."

"You don't like shelters?"

"No."

The conversation went nowhere. The accountant had a very narrow base. As he saw his job, he was hired to prepare tax returns, not to give tax-planning or investment advice. He wasn't really qualified to do that, and in fact the whole idea of it frightened him. But Nancy and Eric, like so many people, somehow assumed that their accountant would advise them. They confused a simple suggestion from him — "Be sure and save all your business-related receipts. We can deduct those, even if it's a dinner you give in your own home

. . . If you have a business trip to Florida and tack a week of vacation on the end of it, we can still deduct a good part of the trip as a business expense . . ."

That sort of thing is pretty standard advice from accountants, and to unsophisticated people it seems like great wisdom and real tax shrewdness. Whatever it is, it isn't financial planning, and you confuse the two at your peril.

Accountants make referrals to me, and I'm happy to have the business. At times the advice I give their referrals is so simple, they could have given it themselves, I'm sure, but they just don't want to stick their necks out.

I had a case like that — Mr. Edwards, a very wealthy man in his eighties. He lived a simple life, had a stock portfolio worth $1.25 million and $1 million in Treasury bills.

He didn't want to touch his stocks. They weren't bad and he was in love with each and every one. He wanted to know what else I could do for him, especially about the amount of taxes he was paying.

All the dividends on his stocks were fully taxable, and so was all the interest on his Treasury bills. He reached the 50% federal, 14% New York State and 4.3% New York City brackets (although his Treasury bills were free of state and city taxes).

Since he wouldn't let me touch his stocks, I took the entire $1 million of Treasuries and put them into tax-exempt bonds. We saved all the taxes he had been paying on the return from the T bills, which had been about $100,000 a year.

Now, that to me was all pretty simple, and I wondered at first why the accountant himself hadn't done it. But I realized in one conversation with him that even the shift from T bills frightened him, since there is nothing as safe as they are. Further, it wasn't his business to know one tax-free bond from another. What I did was put Mr. Edwards into municipal bonds with good ratings and excellent safety features —

not equal to T bills, but extremely high quality bonds nonetheless. The accountant couldn't have made such a choice.

Buying insurance is not financial planning. I am a financial planner. I am also an insurance broker. I know the difference between the two jobs. An awful lot of people get fooled by their insurance broker into thinking that he's producing a whole financial plan for them when all he's doing is selling them more insurance.

One basic law when it comes to insurance, which we'll explore in Chapter 14: What you need for insurance varies at different times of your life.

Recently I cut the life insurance coverage on one man in half because his plan had been conceived years ago, when he was the sole source of income for his wife and two small children. The children had both since finished college and were working. His true needs — or those of his wife if he died — were vastly reduced.

Second incomes. More than half the women in America today are working. At times I find that couples are blind to the facts of that second income, as if it's found money. They don't bear in mind the taxes related to that income or the expenses involved in earning it: clothing, child care, commuting fare, lunches.

I think that a couple's attitude toward the second income is a reflection of the degree of liberation the woman and her husband have. If they respect her $20,000 just as much as they do his $40,000, then they treat it the same way. Most of my clients do.

Living risk-free. I touched on this in the previous chapter, but it cannot be stressed enough: All investments entail risks. There is no such thing as a risk-free life. We have to consider how much you can make on a particular investment, how much you can lose, what has happened in crucial stretches of our history.

Some of my clients are old enough to remember the Depression very well. That's an instructive period of time. During it, a lot of people lost a lot of money in real estate. I remind clients of that when they tell me that they only feel safe if their money is in real estate. I remind them also of our recession of 1974–75, when real property dropped 20% in value.

Similarly, many people have the impression that bonds are always safer than stocks. But if interest rates rise, bonds fall in price. If you have to sell your bonds, you might get only a portion of their value. In the 1960s, 6% or thereabouts was a good rate on a tax-exempt bond. In 1981, a lot of people were holding 6% tax-exempt bonds that had been bought at par (100) in 1965, but they were now trading at a price of, say, 60, which meant $600 on a thousand. You could get 12% on new tax-exempt bonds at that time in the market. So if you needed cash and had to sell that 6% bond at that time, you can see you'd be losing almost 40% of your investment. And if you held on to the bonds, your 6% return wasn't even matching inflation.

That's another risk with bonds. You lock yourself into a fixed rate for a long, long time. When you buy, the rate might seem adequate to more than cover inflation. But we have seen in the last ten years what can happen.

I try to explain that we are faced with risk wherever we turn, but we can deal with that. Real estate can fluctuate in price, although it is fair to say that, in general, real property is less risky than stocks. Common stocks are among the riskiest investments, and they also give you a chance at the biggest profits.

Tangible things are inherently less risky than pieces of paper. Bonds can be risky, especially long-term bonds, as we've seen. They can also be sad surprises. What bondholder

in Penn Central ever dreamed that company would go bankrupt? Until Cleveland and New York City, Chrysler and
Lockheed, all in recent years, who would ever have second
thoughts about the relative safety of such bond issuers?

Risk versus balance. We can control risk by balancing our
investments, by going into several areas.

Take the bond risk. A man of some means with rather
conservative tendencies came to me recently. The first obvious move was to put him into tax-exempt bonds. He was
interested in some that were paying 10½%, maturing in 2012.
I didn't like that risk. We had just come through a period in
which interest rates had gone to 18%, 20%. Though I didn't
think we were about to see such a surge again, I didn't want
the man exposed to a loss in which his bonds could be selling
for 50¢ on the dollar. We were talking about investing $100,-
000.

I considered another route — buying bonds that would
mature in two or three years. Even if they did drop some in
price, they'd mature so quickly that all he'd have to do to
protect his investment was to hold them to maturity, and he'd
have his money with no loss. The catch with these was yield.
Since the risk was so low, the return was low, about 6%.
That's especially bad when faced with an inflation rate of
at least 6½%.

So I decided to buy longer-term bonds, but in a mixed bag.
I bought five-year bonds, fifteen-year bonds and thirty-year
bonds. That gave us protection because we knew that if he
needed cash, he'd always have something at or close to maturity and he wouldn't have to sell off long-term bonds and eat
a loss. I also took some of his money and put it into an annuity, which paid him 12% interest, without current taxes,
and couldn't go down in price.

What we ended up with were bonds, which made him comfortable, and balance, which made me comfortable.

Allow me one of Cohen's Laws: It is far better to be very aggressive with your investments and hedge them by diversification than to be conservative and put all your eggs in one supposedly safe basket. You're going to do much better if you buy six or seven aggressive stocks than if you buy one conservative stock. How do you limit your risk? By buying several different kinds of stocks, say a mix of electronics, drugs, retailing, computers. More on this later when we get into stock market investing.

CHAPTER 4

Taxes and investments: How to make an honest buck in the market and get to keep it

GENE ROBINSON sincerely loved the stock market. He loved picking winners, sometimes based on tips and rumors, sometimes on his own analysis of stocks filtered through the fad market wisdom of the moment. His passion was fed by his brother-in-law, who was a stockbroker, and not a bad one at that. The year before Robinson came to me, he made $20,000 from his stocks.

A nice profit, on the surface at least, and it came on top of a substantial salary. As the vice-president of a chemical company in Houston, Robinson earned $105,000 a year, plus a bonus of $20,000.

He came to see me during one of his frequent business trips to New York, and doing so was something of an act of courage for him. After all, he was the financial vice-president and controller of his company, which meant he was in charge of its money.

"I think I know some things about money," he told me, "but something's wrong with my personal business. I'm making real good money, Mr. Cohen, but I can't seem to put my hands on much of it."

I told him not to be embarrassed, his situation was familiar to me. Watching the cash flow of his chemical company, ar-

ranging the best line of credit with a bank, had little to do
with managing his own money affairs.

"I didn't tell my brother-in-law I was coming to see you,"
he said, smiling. "Silly, I suppose, but I didn't want an argument with him. He's a real smart broker, and he sort of con-
siders himself my financial adviser."

"Advising you about stocks and planning your finances
can be two very different things," I said.

"In all fairness to him," he replied, "he's hardly ever put
me in a dog, and as a decent brother-in-law he doesn't churn
my account" (buying and selling for no purpose except to
build up his commissions).

"I can see he's good," I told him. "You took $20,000 out
of the market last year."

He nodded. "That's part of my problem."

"Making that kind of money?" I asked, confused.

"Watching it vanish," he replied. "We've been averaging
a profit of 15 or 20% on my stocks. And yet. . ."

"Mr. Robinson, I've got news for you. Twenty percent isn't
enough."

"C'mon. I got plenty of friends. They see their stocks go
up 10%, 15%, they sell. Take their money and run."

"Then they're even worse off than you are. Forget the 20%
profit you're taking on a stock. Look at your true rate of
return."

He had brought his tax returns from the previous three
years. At a glance I could see that he was in the 50% bracket
and that's where his trouble started. Because he loved to play
the market, loved the action of picking one stock, watching
it rise, selling it off, he never held on to a stock very long.
That meant that all of his profits were "short-term capital
gains"; he owned the stocks less than one year. On that basis,
his profits were taxed just as if they were salary, which is to
say at the highest possible rate. My hope was to get Robinson
to understand that unless we did something about that, he

was always going to share everything with his silent partner, Uncle Sam — his silent, *equal* partner.

I did the cold arithmetic for him. "You say you're earning a 20% profit. But in your tax bracket, 50%, we've got to figure that half that profit goes right to the IRS. Which means you're down to a 10% profit on those stocks. You pay no state income tax in Texas, so we don't have to knock your profit down even more. But we do have to figure inflation. Let's assume it might be 6%. When you apply that to your shrunken profit, you are down to a true rate of return, Mr. Robinson, I'm sad to say, of 4%."

"That's simply awful," he said.

"Not only awful," I told him, "it doesn't make any sense. For a measly return like that, you shouldn't be in the stock market at all. It isn't worth the risk."

"It's all in those damn taxes," he said.

"Not all," I replied, "but that's where we start and where we keep coming back to."

We took his tax returns and began to analyze them.

In addition to his own income of $125,000, Robinson's wife earned $18,000 as a grade-school teacher. And she contributed more than $10,000 to the family from interest on bonds that she owned, a gift from her parents when she and Gene married.

He had his aggressive common stock action, which brought them $20,000 in profits, as well as $4000 from dividends on the stocks he owned. He had about $100,000 of stock in his portfolio, of which his "equity," or what he owned outright, was $60,000; the remaining $40,000 was "margin," in effect a loan from his brother-in-law's brokerage house. Like any loan, he was paying interest on the margin account, and it came to $4600. It was all deductible from his taxes.

The Robinsons owned some property near Santa Fe, on which they intended to build a vacation home. But as yet they did nothing with it except pay local taxes of $700. The property was worth about $25,000 and rising in value steadily.

Same for their home. It was now worth about $170,000. They bought it some fifteen years ago for $50,000, still carried an 8% mortgage and owed $20,000 on it.

Altogether the Robinsons and their two sons, aged twelve and fifteen, who earned nothing but occasional pocket money, showed income of more than $175,000.

Their deductions included the $4600 interest on the margin account and some $15,000 from other Schedule A items on their tax return, such as sales tax and charitable contributions; and $2400 of mortgage interest and real estate taxes. Their personal exemptions came to $4000. Or a total of $26,000 in deductions and exemptions.

This left them with $149,000 of net taxable income, which put them in the 50% bracket. Their federal income tax amounted to about $58,000.

"I really need a tax shelter, don't I?" Robinson asked.

Like so many people, when he thought about cutting down his income taxes, he thought first and foremost of a shelter. "You need a lot of things," I told him. "A shelter is one of them, but the last one we should think about. First I've got to design ways you can invest your money and not pay taxes on your interest and profits."

"I'm fascinated," Robinson said. "Wave your wand."

I started with his wife's bonds. The problem was common. Robinson and his wife had been given a generous marriage gift years ago, a bunch of bonds that at the time were worth about $140,000. Like most people, they looked at bonds as if they were evergreen trees: They didn't need much attention, and year after year they were there, and year after year they yielded a steady return. There were American Tel & Tel paying 6% a year, Exxon paying 6.5% and Houston Lighting and Power 7.5%. There were six other issues in the package — a couple of major industrial companies, the rest utilities.

"Got to sell these bonds," I told Robinson.

He looked surprised. "That's like killing a pet dog," he said.

"Don't make me a murderer. We've got two big problems with these things. First, they're producing $10,000-plus in income for you, and every penny of it is taxable. We've got to get you tax-free income. Also, we should sell because their value has dropped so. They used to be worth $140,000. Today we can only get something like $100,000 for them.

"You think it's good business to lose $40,000?"

"We'll take it as a tax loss and use it to write off against your stock market gains. Your alternative is to hold these things until they mature, all of them around the year 2000. At that point you'll get the full $140,000 on the bonds. But when you think about the taxes you're going to continue paying on their income each year, that nice steady $10,000, and when you think about inflation and what that $140,000 will really be worth in the year 2000, we're much better off selling now and making a kind of swap."

As I explained to Robinson, once we sold the bonds, we had both a $40,000 loss that we could apply against his market gains and $100,000 cash. There were a number of tax-smart things we could do with the $100,000.

Conceivably we could put the whole bundle into "tax-exempt bonds." These are simply bonds that are sold by states, local governments, or state and local agencies — not the federal government — and they are not taxed by the Feds. The only tax you might face on these is a state tax if you buy the bonds of a state you don't live in. If you live in a state that has an income tax, you should buy bonds issued in that state. (In many states you may also buy Puerto Rico bonds and not be taxed.) That makes you exempt from state as well as federal taxes. In Texas, Robinson didn't have that problem. With no state tax to worry about, he could buy any tax-exempts.

Another possibility might be a "tax-exempt bond trust." This is a package of bonds, and it works like a mutual fund does with common stocks: Instead of buying particular bonds, you're buying units of the trust.

I like these for someone who needs the tax benefits but doesn't need the current income and who is something of a gambler, like Robinson. The very structure of the trust tends to keep you out of temptation. It allows you to take your yearly earnings and reinvest the money in your trust, let it build and compound itself. You can't readily do that with regular tax-exempt bonds.

We also had the choice of buying some public utility stocks. With these, we wouldn't avoid taxes altogether, but we could defer them. The law allows you to earn up to $750 a year for yourself from public utility dividends (or for a couple up to $1500) and not have to pay any tax on them so long as you reinvest those dividends in additional shares of the utility. Many utilities have plans that qualify, and they can be good, conservative investments.

What I recommended to Robinson was that with the $100,-000 we'd get for his wife's bond portfolio, we should put $15,000 into a public utility stock paying 10%, which would give us $1500 tax-deferred.

The balance, $85,000, I'd put into a tax-exempt bond trust and let it compound.

"Supposing we need some of that money?" he asked.

"You can stop reinvesting the interest at any time, or you can cash in what you have accumulated in the reinvestment account if you want."

He nodded a few times slowly, then sighed. "I have to talk to my wife," he said. "I manage our affairs, but these bonds were really given to her, and I just don't feel right selling them off. She's not only attached to them, like a silver tray we were given at our wedding, but she's so proud of the income they bring us."

"Yeah, but it's taxable income. I explained that to you."
I regretted the words as soon as I said them. It's a problem I
have. Sometimes things seem so clear to me, I can't understand why somebody else doesn't feel the same way I do.

Robinson gave me the sharp look I deserved. "Mr. Cohen,
I know that and, Mr. Cohen, you know that. But to my wife,
it's $10,000 she's contributing to our lives. You know what
that means?"

I cannot tell you the number of times I have given extremely sound advice and had it rejected for personal reasons.

And I thought, when Robinson left my office that day, that
it was about to happen again — even though he said he'd be
in touch after discussing everything with his wife.

"Fine," I told him. "And of course if you'd like me to go
through anything with her, just let me know."

He nodded and continued to pull his papers together.

"You have thoughts about what we can do with my stocks
as well?" he asked.

"I certainly do."

He shook his head. "God, I didn't think this whole thing
was going to get so sticky."

"How so?"

"First I've got to work this out nicely with my wife. Then
my brother-in-law."

I knew I would never hear from him again.

CHAPTER 5

More on taxes and investments and keeping an honest buck

SOME WEEKS LATER, to my surprise, I got a call from Robinson. He was back in New York and wanted to see me, if possible, that afternoon. I restrained myself, but I was bursting to find out what had happened back home in Houston.

He came to my office about four, and as he lowered his body into the stuffed chair across from my desk, he spoke the words I almost said: "Thought you'd never see me again, Mr. Cohen, I'm sure."

"Mr. Robinson, you couldn't be more right."

He wiped his forehead with a large hand. "Mr. Cohen, sir, all I can tell you is it wasn't easy."

As we had both anticipated, his wife had been stunned by my plan. So he had spent evenings giving her a crash course on their problem — too much taxable income — and why one of the solutions centered on her sweet old bonds.

"Actually," he said, "all this stuff isn't that complicated. Except an awful lot of people have a big block in their minds about it. Especially women like my wife, who never dealt with any money stuff more complex than a monthly bank statement. At first, when I'd explain our situation, she'd get headaches. Just get up from the living room sofa and say, 'This is too confusing. I need an aspirin.'" He paused. "Finally, though, I got to give her credit. She came to understand pretty well. And I got to tell you, Mr. Cohen, I feel good that we did it that way instead of my just being high-handed, saying, 'Don't worry about this none, Annie, I'm just making a few sharp moves in the market.'"

"Mr. Robinson, I'm delighted. Both with your approach and your results. I assume we can go ahead now and sell those bonds?"

He nodded. "My bank will transfer them to you. Let's sell them, take the $40,000 loss as a tax write-off, put $15,000 into a good public utility — you might consider Texas Utilities — and get our tax-deferred $1500 return each year. And much as it hurts me to say it, put the remaining $85,000 into one of those boring, boring tax-exempt bond trusts."

I chuckled, took a breath and asked the question: "And everything went as well with your brother-in-law?"

Robinson winced. "I didn't have the heart, Mr. Cohen, or the strength."

I threw up my hands. "It's your money, Mr. Robinson."

"And my taxes," he said. "Maybe we could talk about it a little. It'd help me if I could get a sense of what you might do with my dreadful stock portfolio, if I ever could bring my-self to take it away from my brother-in-law."

"Remember, I had no quarrel with what he did, except that everything was a short-term capital gain, everything was bought and sold in less than a year, and you simply can't take the tax rap that comes with that."

"I understand, I understand. Give me strategy."

"Just before we get into that, let me give you a piece of good news, Mr. Robinson."

"Yes?"

"I've just made you $15,700."

I watched the grin slowly spread across his face, joy and surprise mingled in his expression.

"Mr. Cohen, you just explain about the $15,700 and you won't even have to tell me the rest of the strategy."

"A pleasure," I said, and it was. "You made $20,000 in the market, plus about $10,600 on bond interest. The IRS got half of all that, leaving you with $15,300. That's the way it used to be."

He nodded.

"But now we have a tax loss on the bonds we're selling, and it's more than the gain on your stocks. The law allows us to apply that loss against your gain. Now there'll be no tax on your stock profits. Your $20,000 will really be $20,000, not $10,000. In addition, we're switching your taxable bonds to tax-frees. The tax-frees and the utility dividends will earn you about $9500 a year."

"That's $29,500," Robinson said, "compared with $15,300 the old way."

"Right, and that's not all. The government says you must apply $6000 of a long-term loss against $3000 of ordinary income when you file your taxes. So we deduct $3000 from your income and that saves us another $1500 in taxes. Altogether, then, we have $31,000, compared with $15,300 the old way. A net benefit to you of $15,700."

"I love it," said Robinson, "just love it."

I went on to review the arithmetic of his taxes. This year he'll show a loss on the bonds of $40,000, of which we'll apply $20,000 against his stock profit and $6000 against salaried income. The tax law permits him to "carry forward" the balance, a $14,000 loss he can use on next year's tax return.

Next year, $6000 of that $14,000 could go to reduce his earned income by $3000 again, but it would be better if he makes $14,000 in the market. Then he can apply his $14,000 "carry-forward," and his $14,000 market profits will not be taxed, whether they are short or long term.

"But that'll be the last of our free ride with tax losses," I told him. "Now we want a new investment policy."

"To start with," I went on, "we'll try to make each stock investment a long-term capital gain. I know we won't be able to do that every time, because with a very aggressive stock account we'll have to take short-term gains now and then. But we'll try. The important thing to bear in mind is that you can't keep buying and selling every time the market has an upward blip. And these days, with hundred-point swings in the market, the temptation to grab your profit and run, no matter how long you've owned the stock, can be overwhelming. Especially for a player like yourself."

As I explained to Robinson, I consider long-term capital gains something of a tax shelter, though not in the common use of that term. But look at it this way: What the tax law says is, "Hold that stock for a year and a day, and you will have 60% of your profit not touched by taxes at all. On the remaining 40%, you pay at your highest bracket." So, 50% bracket, you end up paying half of 40%, or what amounts to 20% of your total profit. If you're in the 40% bracket, your tax will be that much lower, amounting to only 16% of your long-term gain.

Compare that with the way Robinson was paying. On his short-term gains, he was paying nearly 50% of his profit in federal taxes. Nothing was spared. Any time I can get away with a tax of only 20% rather than 50%, I've "sheltered" some of my money.

"What about that temptation you talk about?" Robinson asked. "I mean, it's something fierce these days, watching that Dow-Jones bounce around, fifty points, a hundred points. How in the world can a man sit there and not take his profits, taxes be damned?"

"Ever heard of mutual funds?"

"Mutual funds," he said, scorn in his voice. "God, you do come up with the dullest ideas."

Another sigh, another leap. In a way Robinson was right. There's nothing very exciting about parking your money in a mutual fund, where a lot of anonymous managers can move it around. Still, mutuals can be extremely useful vehicles, especially for someone like Robinson.

They can curb temptation and they can cut taxes. I look

at them, I told him, as engines that can generate long-term capital gains. The fund is able to buy and sell every day, taking full advantage of shifts in the market, yet all the short-term action wouldn't have any tax consequences for him. Indeed, the most successful funds in recent years have been ones that actively turn over their portfolios. The great tax difference here would be that Robinson wouldn't be buying stocks directly, he'd be buying shares in the fund. No matter what the fund did with its seventy-five or a hundred stocks, no matter how many times it bought and sold, so long as he held his shares in the fund for a year and a day, he could then sell them and take a long-term capital gain.

"I suppose you're right," he allowed. "They could be useful. Though I must confess, I honestly believe I could pick stocks as well as any mutual fund, Mr. Cohen."

"That may be," I told him, "and I feel the same way. But that's not the point here, is it?"

"True, true," he agreed, a bit sadly. "I suppose you've got a few favorites?"

I told him I liked the Oppenheimer group, whose growth funds had been outstanding in recent years. The Putnam group and Lord Abbott had also been good.

"They're all no-loads, I assume?"

"Never. You pay a fee for each. I don't know a no-load I trust."

A "load" fund is one where you pay up to 8.5% commission when you buy your shares of it, nothing when you sell them. "No-load" funds charge no commission, and Robinson was like countless other clients who simply assume there is no point in paying a fat commission if you don't have to.

"Seems to me, Mr. Cohen, with all due respect, I've heard of several no-loads with spectacular performance records."

"True, and I still won't buy them." My problem with them starts with the fact that for the most part, no-loads are small organizations dependent on the skills of one or two people.

They might be smart, maybe even lucky, and have a spectacular streak for a couple of years. That's not enough for me.

"If I recommend a fund to you, Mr. Robinson, I want a large, substantial organization, not dependent on the abilities of any one person. That guy gets hit by a bus, you lose."

"My problem is, Mr. Cohen, that deep down I guess I really want to be that one guy. Before he gets hit by the bus, of course."

I went on to tell him that beyond errant buses, I worried about any fund with a single philosophy and view of the market. "Nobody's got all the answers, even though there are plenty of gurus around who claim they do."

Another problem with no-loads was that they normally aren't big enough or diversified enough for me. "I want a family of funds to switch you around. At least four or five different funds. We start out putting everything in their most aggressive fund and the market begins to collapse, I want to move you — for a $5 fee or something like that — into their money market fund. Wait out the storm."

I also needed an organization that was regularly introducing new funds. Very successful funds get too attractive and then get too big. After a certain point, their size limits their action. They can only buy the giant stocks, Exxon, GM, duPont. For their economics to make sense, they have to buy such a large dollar amount of a stock that they can't go near small companies. If they like a small company and buy $50,000 worth of the stock, what effect would that have on a fund with net assets of $1 billion, even if the stock doubled?

Regarding performance, I told Robinson that he was right, certain no-loads had done very well. You will always find a couple of them near the top of the performance charts. But you won't find any that have been at the top consistently for the past fifteen years. Unfortunately, doing what most people do, which is to look at some kind of current hit parade of funds, doesn't provide any perspective. I need the long view.

I want to be able to evaluate funds in relation to market cycles. I can think of four or five no-loads which are doing well now but which were total disasters in 1973 and 1974.

Yet those are benchmark years for me. We had a severe bear market during that time, and I want to know just how far down a mutual fund went then. I won't buy a fund that leaves you that vulnerable in a bear market. I believe and hope that I can move my clients into a money market fund before a market disaster occurs. Up to now my timing has been good. Most recently I was out of the market for mutual fund clients during the 1981–82 bear market, and I was back in by the summer of 1982. Good timing, and it allowed my people to earn 50% on their money in the first six months of the soaring bull market of 1982–83.

But I can't guarantee that will always happen. I want my clients, in that case, to have the added security of a fund's track record, which at least suggests that if the market takes a disastrous drop and we fail to get out, the fund will have defensive characteristics built in for protection. The fund will go down, of course. But if the market drops 20%, I don't want a fund whose track record indicates that it could drop 60%. The fund should drop not much more than the market drops, even though it went up much more than the market went up. There are funds with records like that, and nearly all of them are load funds.

"That all makes good sense, Mr. Cohen," Robinson said, "but I'd still like to do something about that commission. Having to pay anybody 8½% is too painful. Couldn't that be negotiated?"

"It is high, I agree. And there is a way to cut it down, a kind of built-in discount. What they call 'breakpoints.' The more you invest with them, the less commission you have to pay."

The breakpoint is the investment amount at which the load decreases. Typically, with a $10,000 investment, the load will drop to 7½%. At $25,000, it'll go down to 6%. And so on, dropping again at $50,000 and $100,000. I simply don't think 6% is an excessive amount to be paying for the service and expertise you get.

Also, it is usually possible to combine investments to hit breakpoints. You might have your IRA as one account in a family of funds, your personal account as another, something for your child as a third, but you can usually combine all the accounts to cut down your load charge.

Most of the funds will also give you a lower rate if you intend to reach a certain higher level of investment. Say you open your fund account with $10,000 and you expect to invest another $15,000 in the next thirteen months. You sign a note to that effect, and they charge you the percentage rate they would if you had put in $25,000 at the start. If you aren't able to invest the intended extra $15,000, they simply recalculate the whole deal. No penalties to you, and the chance of saving a chunk of the fee.

Nowadays some no-loads are becoming low-loads. The successful ones are starting to charge 2% or 3%. That's less than a load fund, but in the long run it could be more. Most load fund groups will let you switch in and out of their funds without additional charges. Say you buy Putnam Vista fund with $10,000. You'll pay a load at the reduced rate of 7½%. If the $10,000 grows to $13,000 and you think the market is starting to look shaky, switch into Putnam's money market fund. There you might pick up $400 or so of interest income, and then if the market seems better, you switch back into Vista fund with $13,400. That switch costs you just $5. You can't do that with low-load funds. Usually they have no grouping of accounts, no breakpoints and no free reentry.

I guess Robinson and I had been talking for almost an hour when he held up his hand. "Mr. Cohen," he said, "I gotta stop you. I'm feeling guilty taking up more of your time."

"I don't follow," I replied. "I'm happy to take whatever time we have to, to get the right plan for you."

He shook his head. "No need. I see where your plan is leading. I mean, there's nothing you've said so far that doesn't make sense. Don't take offense, Mr. Cohen, you sure know your business."

"Then what's the problem?"

"You're going to take all my fun away."

"You think I'm going to say, 'Let's take your whole portfolio, $100,000 worth of stocks, sell them and put all your money into mutual funds'?"

He nodded. "Alas, Mr. Cohen, that is exactly where you are leading me. And I know you're the doctor. But if I can't have any fun, what's the point? I mean, Mr. Cohen, like I said, I really love to play the market."

"Okay, I hear you, Mr. Robinson. Maybe we can work out a compromise. I mean, I can't sit here and let you continue investing the way you have been. That's crazy. Coughing up half of it to the government. Taking the risks you do for about a 4% true net profit. Crazy."

"I'm a businessman, Mr. Cohen. I understand the word *compromise*. Talk to me."

"Let's start with your kids," I said.

"My kids?" he said, sitting forward and smiling, genuine surprise in his voice. "Mr. Cohen, I like your moves."

Up to this point, we had not mentioned his two teenaged boys, but I had been wondering if there wasn't some way we could deflect some of Robinson's earnings onto them. At present, they earned nothing, paid zero taxes. If we could shift income onto them, they would have to pay taxes on it, but at low, low rates.

I suggested to Robinson that we set up a brokerage account for each boy, putting $20,000 in each. By law they would have to be regular cash accounts, since "margin" is not allowed for "custodial accounts" such as these.

If we did that, beyond dealing with part of Robinson's in-

vestment problem, we'd get started with some broader planning that he had neglected up to then: We'd start college
funds for the boys.

Of course, we could be more conservative with the kids,
putting them into a bond trust rather than stocks. Either way
we'd be deflecting earnings and taxes onto them, relieving
Robinson of those taxes.

"So far so good," he said. "Very good. What about the rest
of the money? We've got maybe another $60,000 to play
with."

"I'd put $25,000 into what you call one of those boring
mutual funds."

"I'm not impressed."

"And with the remaining $35,000, I'd set up a margin ac-
count. With the margin, you'd borrow another $35,000 from
my brokerage house and have $70,000 to invest in the market.
Notice, Mr. Robinson, I try to use the word *invest*."

"Mr. Cohen, you're making a believer of me. Yessir, I'm
going to stop 'playing the market.' From here on in, I am an
investor." He spoke the last word softly, as if to impart special dignity to it.

"You're giving me a hard time, Mr. Robinson, but it's
okay if you mean it."

"Cross my heart, Mr. Cohen, on my mother's grave." He
crossed his heart and smiled broadly.

"And I want you to make me a promise."

"Anything."

"You invest with two things in mind."

"And those are, sir?"

"Listening, as tough as it might be, to my advice so you
can pick stocks intelligently."

"Go on."

"Trying for long-term capital gains on all your investments,
whether they're stocks from me or ones you select from one
of your own infallible systems."

"How can we lose?"

"We can't. Not if you do that."

"And just supposing, Mr. Cohen, my flesh is weak. I suc-
cumb to temptation and I make a killing. Only it's a stupid
killing because it's a short-term gain. I suppose then we're
right back where we started when I first came to you, with me
having to give half of it to the Feds."

"Not necessarily," I told him. "We might be able to find
you a tax shelter in that case. But rather than talk about that
maneuver or even think about it, let us trust to the strength
of your newfound faith."

"Amen, Mr. Cohen, amen. I even think I may have now
found the strength to confront my venal brother-in-law."

Checklist for Chapters 4 and 5

1. To figure out what percentage you are really earning on
an investment, subtract the percent you will have to pay in
federal as well as state and local taxes. Then subtract the
going rate of inflation, say 6%. What's left is your true rate
of return.

2. Avoid investments in stocks or bonds that bring you
income that will be taxed as "ordinary" income, that is, like
salary, but at your highest tax level.

3. On all stock investments, aim for long-term capital
gains; don't sell a stock unless you have owned it for a year
and a day. By law, 60% of your long-term capital gain is tax-
free. The remaining 40% is taxed at the rate of your highest
bracket, but even if you are in the 50% bracket, you will
still be paying only 20% of your gain in taxes (or 50% of the
remaining, taxable 40%).

4. Anytime you pay taxes on only 40% of a gain rather
than 100%, you have "sheltered" part of your earnings.

5. Consider mutual funds as great vehicles for generating
long-term capital gains. The fund itself might be buying and
selling its stocks every day for short-term gains. But you own

shares of the fund, not individual stocks. So long as you hold your shares for a year and a day, your profit from then on will be a long-term capital gain.

6. To avoid taxable income on bonds, consider tax-free bonds or tax-free bond trusts.

7. Think about setting up custodial accounts for your children. You can manage the accounts, the earnings will go to them and the taxes on those earnings will be at the children's low, low levels, as opposed to your own high one. The result is more money for the family at large and college funds building for your children.

CHAPTER 6

G*etting beyond the myths and magic of tax shelters*

THE CALL came early in November. This one was from Paul Appleton, who taught at the university with my wife. He was a professor of economics, which did not mean he necessarily knew a great deal about personal finances. My wife had mentioned him to me as an example of how to cash in on the prestige of a university position. Appleton had become somewhat famous around the campus as a superconsultant. He counseled banks and insurance companies, casting light on the dark future of the American economy, and he earned more from dispensing such wisdom than he did from being a professor.

As I suggested, not much of his highly paid wisdom extended to his personal money matters, and he was calling me because a friend had pointed out that given the amount of consulting he was doing, he could well end up paying $50,000 in taxes that year.

It was a familiar call and problem, and it came at the usual time of year. Why so many people wake up in November, I don't know. "I think I need a tax shelter," they say. "Help!"

For all his other knowledge, this man knew little about shelters. He didn't know how they really work, or even whether they were suitable to his situation and, if so, which kind of shelter would be best. The word *shelter*, however, was magic to him and that's what he was looking for — some magic to make his taxes go away.

"I'd like to help you, Paul," I told him, "but you're calling me at the worst time of the year. The first half of the year is the time to buy tax shelters," I said. "In fact, the earlier the better. The tax laws won't let you deduct what you don't spend. So a shelter deal that gets started in December doesn't have the time to commit your funds to actual development work. You wouldn't get a big enough write-off this year. Also, I should warn you that there are many scams around in November and December, floated by clever promoters who know that a lot of people like yourself are desperate this time of year."

"I see," he replied. "Well, obviously I don't want any trouble like that, Stanley. I just thought you might know of something that's good and legitimate and, uh, uh — " He paused as if he were checking a note. "— something economically viable?"

Ah, that great phrase, "economically viable." I talked for a while with the professor. It was obvious that he was an intelligent fellow and just as obvious that he did need a shelter. What was especially interesting to me was that through our whole conversation he never used the word *investment*.

But that's what shelters are. They are not mystical devices created by devious congressmen or promoters to cause your taxes to vanish. They are investments that offer you certain tax benefits (those famous write-offs), along with a chance to make a return on your money. There are, after all, two ways to participate in a business. You can buy stock in it, or you can be a direct owner. With a shelter, you become a direct owner, a limited partner. If your company buys equipment and receives an investment tax credit or other benefit, those tax benefits don't flow through to you if you merely own stock in the company. But if you're a limited partner, a proportionate share of those benefits comes to you, and you may apply it against your personal income taxes.

Tax shelters must always be looked at as investments and, as such, be compared with other possible uses for your money. What is your total economic return going to be if you put your money into a real estate shelter? You have to figure out what you gain from write-offs in terms of money that you *won't* have to pay to the IRS, plus income, plus the capital gain you should realize when your real estate project is sold, say, ten years later. And you've also got to figure out the "time value" of the money. How much is the $30,000 you will receive ten years from now worth to you today? After you've considered all these factors, and not just the tax benefits, then you have an intelligent basis on which to decide whether that real estate shelter is a good deal for you.

That's assuming you've made some other calculations and assessments beforehand, because as we'll see later, you should have a clear overview of your entire financial condition before you make any decisions about shelters.

How they work

The two main kinds of shelters are real estate and oil and gas. What makes them shelters, what permits them to offer you tax benefits that other investments may not have, is that they are specially structured to take advantage of the write-offs that the law permits. Some of these write-offs derive from very conventional and ordinary things, such as the interest on mortgages or the depreciation of property. Some are very specialized and involve particular benefits that the federal government provides to people to encourage them to invest in various areas of the economy. For example, if the Feds think it would be good for the country to have more people invest in the preservation of landmark buildings or housing projects for the poor and the elderly, it will allow tax benefits to encourage them to do so.

There are eternal arguments over the philosophy behind shelters: Would it be better to eliminate shelters and have that much more money collected in taxes so that if the government really wanted more housing for old folks, it could build houses with the extra revenue collected?

As times and administrations change, the laws on shelters change. Some write-offs are banned, others are created. But the basic elements and benefits remain.

Take real estate shelters. In a typical deal you might invest anywhere from $35,000 to $75,000, spread over four to six years. You'd start the first year by investing, say, $10,000, then the second year it'd go up to $13,600, the third year drop down to $8200, the fourth year to $5800, the fifth and last year to $4100. You would have sent the general partners of the project a total of $41,700.

Say this deal involves a two-to-one write-off during pay-in, which means that for every dollar you invest, you would deduct roughly two dollars from your federal income tax return. That means you take off $20,000 in the first year, about $27,-000 the second, $17,000 the third and so on.

Let's also say that this deal of yours was launched in June with your first contribution of $10,000. For the second through fifth year, you continue to send in checks, usually in January or February, and over the five-year time span you get a total of about $84,000 in write-offs. If you're in the 50% bracket, that's $42,000 that you save on taxes, $42,000 that you do *not* pay to the IRS, which is obviously one of the happiest attractions of this investment.

In addition, during the next four or five years you will still get tax write-offs, even though you are not paying in any more money. In this case, the additional write-offs might total $35,000, giving you another $17,500 you have saved on taxes.

After a couple of years, you will start receiving income from the project, but what I'm describing is a highly subsidized real estate offering with large write-offs, and the income from this sort of deal is usually very small, maybe only a few hundred dollars a year. Perhaps along about the eighth or ninth year, when your write-offs have dwindled to very small amounts and you are approaching the dreaded "crossover" point (of which we'll speak later), your general partner will be looking to sell the project.

If he does sell and make a successful deal, your share could be a capital gain of a sizable amount.

A tax shelter investment in another real estate deal, one that doesn't involve subsidized or government-assisted housing, might be structured in a very similar way. But the write-offs won't be as great, although the income will be much greater and very possibly the capital gain at the end of the whole process will be a larger one.

Oil and gas deals typically involve a single lump-sum investment, and if you are in a deal that is established early enough in the year, your write-off will be 100% of what you invest, or very close to it.

Let's say you put $10,000 into an oil and gas public program that is launched in April. Typically, you'll get a write-off of something like $8500. The sponsor's fees, commissions and some other expenses are not deductible, and that's why you don't get a full $10,000 write-off. In a few oil and gas deals, the general partners may advance the money for the fees and then the write-off would be one for one, or a full $10,000 on your $10,000 investment. Some oil and gas deals involve "assessments," which simply means that they'll ask you for maybe $2500 in the second year. If they do, that means they've struck oil and need additional funds to drill more wells at the site. Your deal may involve voluntary second-year contributions or mandatory ones. Either way you'll get a write-off for whatever you put in.

If you've chosen wisely and luckily, your limited partnership hits oil or gas. In the second and following years of the program, you receive regular checks in the mail, your share of the earnings from the wells. Now you get another tax break, from the famous "depletion allowance." Roughly 25% of your income from the wells will be tax-free. The income won't be in steady amounts, because oil wells pump the greatest amount of oil at the outset and gradually taper off. The first four or five years will give you by far the greatest part of the income, and often by the fifteenth year the amount of cash coming back to you will be down to negligible levels. But some wells go right on pumping for as many as thirty or forty years.

When a shelter makes sense and for whom

In Chapter 4, with Gene Robinson from Houston, we saw that his first reaction when I touched the nerve of taxes was to think of shelters, almost reflexively. But as his situation also showed us, there are several techniques for cutting and deferring taxes, and the last one you should use is a tax shelter. It comes *after* we've put you into as many retirement programs as we can, for example, as many tax-free bonds, as many long-term capital gain possibilities and every other device to reduce the taxes on your earnings and to convert your investments from taxable to tax-free or tax-advantaged.

It comes *after* we can see, with all those and other techniques working for us, what your taxes will still amount to. That's essential, because so far as I'm concerned, I don't want you investing in a tax shelter unless you are still, after all other strategies, showing that you have 50%-bracket earnings to protect. Recalling our tax onion from Chapter 1, we are continually peeling away the layers. If all our efforts have peeled you down to, say, the 40% bracket, I don't want you buying any shelters. You should be looking for other kinds of investments.

Quite simply, if you shelter 40% money, you're not getting the most for your money, you're not getting the maximum write-off.

Let's say your boss touts a particular oil and gas shelter. The difference between your boss, whom you want to impress, and yourself is not that he is so much smarter than you, but that he earns more money than you. He is high on this deal because he really has some 50% earnings to shelter, whereas when you are finished with all your deductions and other tax-saving efforts, you're down to 40%. Still, you let appearances and ego intrude, so you also invest $10,000 in the shelter. Better than most of its kind, it allows you a full one-to-one write-off, a full $10,000. For your boss, that means a saving of $5000, or 50% of $10,000. You, however, in your 40% bracket will save only $4000, only four-fifths as much. Which is not known as getting the most for your money. There are better things to do with your $10,000, even if they don't bring you the same tax benefits.

(Generally speaking and throughout this chapter, a tax shelter means the kind of limited partnership that throws off big write-offs. There are in the world of limited partnerships more conservative, lower risk creatures which stress income far more than write-offs, and which might be more suitable to a 40% bracket reader. I'm thinking of something like an oil income fund or a diversified, conventional real estate deal, of which more in Chapter 13.)

Earlier I took special note of the great phrase "economically viable." I don't think a shelter promoter can give you the time of day without adding, "It's economically viable." Applied to a shelter, it means basically that in addition to the tax benefits the deal offers, it is a sound investment in the usual sense of the term. It is not enough, in other words, to receive those write-offs. If you don't also make money on your investment, you have a lousy deal. When the promoter says it's economically viable, he's saying that you should see a fair return on your money.

But there isn't any way that you can put $10,000 into a real estate shelter, deduct $20,000 and then go on to make exactly as much money as you would make on another $10,000 real estate investment that doesn't provide comparable write-offs. If there were a way to do this, then there wouldn't be any conventional real estate business in this country at all. There'd be nothing but tax shelters.

Alas, in the real world you can't have your cake and eat it. You can't have the maximum possible write-off, the maximum income and the maximum capital gain all in the same deal. Shelters are often a trade-off, swapping some big tax advantages up front for a somewhat diminished return on your money later on.

When Congress structures housing laws, it implicitly says, "Here are these nifty tax benefits. We'll give them to you because we want you to have an incentive to build homes for the needy and the elderly. But don't be a pig. Don't expect that we're going to give you these write-offs *and* let you make as much money as you would if you went into an ordinary real estate deal offering minimum shelter benefits."

You might get two-to-one write-offs on your real estate shelter. But the income that housing project throws off may be only a few hundred bucks a year. A commercial real estate developer would leap off his highest building with a return like that. But then, he wouldn't be caring for the lower classes. He'd put up his condos in the most desirable part of town, and if you invested in his project, although you still might receive some tax benefits from depreciation of the buildings and interest paid on the mortgage, they'd be small compared with a sheltered deal. What you would be getting instead from the condo deal is money, income on your investment. And depending upon your financial condition, you might be better off with those earnings than you would be with tax write-offs, especially, as noted, if you're in only a 40% bracket.

64

You have to make a judgment about shelters, then, and
whether they really make sense for you. To be sure, some
people are almost automatic candidates. One is the extremely
big salaried earner, someone drawing more than $150,000.

If you paid more than $30,000 in federal income taxes last
year, you are probably a candidate for a tax shelter. If you
paid between $20,000 and $25,000, you are a potential candidate and might want to give shelters a close scrutiny. If you
paid less than $20,000 to the IRS, you can most likely forget
about tax shelters.

Surely, the most blatant shelter candidate ever to walk
into my office was Gerhardt Schmitz. Gerry was a customs
broker, earning about $20,000 a year clearing goods through
customs until August of 1982, when he became the $5 Million
Man. At thirty-six, Gerry won the big prize in the New York
State Lottery.

In November 1982, a close friend of his, seeing that he
had not done any planning with his new fortune, brought him
to me. Gerry himself, quite intelligent in money matters, was
growing very concerned about taxes.

Pleasant, unassuming, extremely easygoing, Gerry had not
much changed his way of living, still occupied the rent-con-
trolled apartment in Yorkville, the German section of Man-
hattan, that he had shared for years with his parents.

The numbers of his new condition were intriguing, if a
bit troubling, looking at them as I was in the next-to-last
month of the year. For 1982, instead of an income of $20,000,
he was now going to show about $250,000. The $5 million
he had won would be paid to him at the rate of $238,000-plus
a year, every September, for twenty-one years.

Obviously we needed shelter, and bad, but even with the
$5 Million Man I had to figure out just how much. So the
first thing I did was a projection of his taxes for 1982 and
1983. Fortunately the tax law allowed us to do five-year averaging. That gave us a substantial break for 1982, since we

could lump his $250,000 year in with the previous four meager ones. In fact, for anyone who has a huge windfall in a single year, five-year averaging is the single biggest protective device.

Even so, it looked as if Gerry faced a tax bill of $90,000 in the first year, 1982. His deductions were minimal.

Making matters worse, I couldn't simply put him into shelters that would give him $90,000 worth of losses for 1982.

Remember, we were at the end of the year. The write-offs he would receive that year would be limited. Just as I told Professor Paul Appleton, you can only write off what the shelter spends, and in two months it wouldn't be able to spend very much.

Further, I had to think beyond 1982. I couldn't load him up with so much shelter in 1982 that he'd be damaged in 1983. Whatever payments he'd make in 1982 for a real estate shelter, for example, would only increase in 1983. And maybe he'd be top-heavy, have more write-offs than he could properly use.

We bought four units of a real estate shelter that gave him about a two-to-one write-off. The first year he contributed $18,000, received a deduction of $37,000. The next year he'd pay $35,000 and receive a $64,000 write-off. Over five years he would invest $134,400 and see deductions of $257,284.

We also bought $10,000 worth of an oil and gas shelter, which gave him $4500 in deductions the first year and more the second.

And we ended up buying all of this, and signing all the documents and checks, over Thanksgiving weekend. Allow me one piece of special advice: Do not close shelter deals over a Thanksgiving weekend. While everyone else in New York City was enjoying family turkeys and the Macy's parade, I was going crazy trying to find a notary. The documents had to be notarized. I finally located one who used to work for my firm, and yes, thank heaven, she had her stamp at home.

All we had to do was go to her apartment, which was on the other side of town from the big parade. All we had to do was get through the parade. Hours later our taxi got there. The $5 Million Man, I learned, is a very nice guy, but he pays taxes just like the rest of us mortals and he can't fly.

Life's happy surprises

Unplanned, happy developments can force us to reach out for shelter in a hurry.

As I told Mr. Robinson, and as we'll see in other parts of the book, I'm always trying for long-term capital gains in the stock market. But there are times when you simply cannot hold a stock for a year and a day, when the thing takes off and all the evidence tells you that if you don't sell now — even if you've held it only four months and will have to pay taxes on it at your highest bracket rate — you're going to lose your gains. You take the short-term gain and must do something so you don't have to share 50% of that (say, a quick $20,000) with the Feds.

Or you have the kind of wonderful fortune that Jan and Mike Mulloy recently had. Both in their early thirties, they live in Chevy Chase, work in Washington. She is a saleswoman with a computer-systems company and he works in public relations, lobbying for a major defense contractor. She was earning $30,000 a year, he $40,000 when they first came to me, and within a year we had a happy problem.

Jan landed a gigantic contract. After two years of planning and selling, she finally sold a government agency on her system. Her income as a result was about to triple to $90,000, and that was only the beginning. She had sold them a five-year contract, so her subsequent years' income would be just as high.

Within a month it was Mike's turn. Quite unexpectedly,

one of his competitors offered him a bigger title and an increase in salary from $40,000 to $55,000 to help them sell military equipment to the Pentagon.

Overnight Jan and Mike went from joint earnings of $70,-000 to $145,000, with reasonably good assurance that future income would be as high or higher. In fact, given the kind of people they were, I knew they'd always be in the 50% bracket. I put them, for starters, into a real estate shelter, to which they would contribute a total of $50,000 over five years and realize tax deductions of more than $100,000 during that period.

I had a similar situation with the Proctors. In their case she had stopped working as a teacher to become a full-time mother. He was an executive in the furniture business earning $60,000, and that plus some interest on investments was what they showed for income.

When the kids reached eleven and fourteen, Dorothy Proctor decided to go back to work. She was certified, had seniority and was able to teach at $28,000 a year. In the same year Norman received and accepted a new job, raising his salary from $60,000 to $85,000.

They have practically doubled their earnings, going from $60,000-plus to $113,000-plus in a year.

With them I used an oil and gas income shelter to cope with two of their planning concerns.

First they had the write-off, about $25,000 on their $30,000 investment. They needed that in their first year at the $113,-000 level.

Then we set things up to make a gift of their shelter to their children. We'll consider this strategem in detail in Chapter 15, but basically it meant that the write-offs on the tax shelter went to Mr. and Mrs. Proctor and the income from the oil wells went to the children. When that income started to come in, the taxable portion of it would be taxed at the kids' very low tax brackets and not at the rate of the parents.

Also, this gave us a way of building up a fund to pay for the children's college years down the road.

The plain and fancy risks of shelters

Up to this point, except for a reference to "clever promoters" who show their faces late in the year and an ominous-sounding "crossover," I've hardly even suggested that shelters are less than perfect creations. In fact, shelters can be risky, but to understand the risks I think it's best to label them X-rated or PG (as recommended for Parental Guidance). By X-rated I mean the ones that give shelters a bad name, the more exotic and ingenious scams. PGs are more mundane deals that need close scrutiny but might be worth your while.

Let's start with the juicier X-rateds and the general observation that enormous ingenuity and energy have gone into devising shelter scams.

There were those film deals where promoters would find some dreadful movie made in Europe that had absolutely no chance of appealing to any conceivable audience in the United States. They would buy the U.S. rights from the European producers and agree to pay them, say, $1 million. Payment would be $100,000 in cash, with the balance of $900,000 an IOU to be paid out of the earnings of the film.

Then the promoters would sell this package as a shelter. As an investor, you, along with others, would put up $10,000 to cover the $100,000 going partly to the Europeans, partly to the heavy expenses and fees of the packagers.

They would arrange for distribution of the film, usually in ratty theaters where the chance of an audience was nil. But at least they could show the IRS that they had certainly tried to sell tickets and had failed.

That failure meant that they never would have to pay off the $900,000 IOU, since it was tied to earnings. Nevertheless, according to the promoters, you could consider your loss on

the basis of the whole package, or $1 million. For your $10,-
000, you would end up with write-offs of something like
$50,000 and more on such deals, five-to-one and even greater.

There were phony art deals where you bought a master-
piece from the shelter promoter for $20,000 and contributed
it to a museum. The promoter was also the link to the museum, and he provided you with an evaluation of the great
work at $150,000.

There were also oilfields that didn't exist, except on the
maps the promoter showed you. The Home Stake scam sucked
in extremely sophisticated money managers and their famous
and rich movie-star clients. For this one the packagers even
provided helicopter trips so that investors could fly over their
soon-to-be-pumping oilfields and see the pretty red, orange
and yellow pipeline winking up at them from the ground.

As the frauds were exposed and the ersatz write-offs disallowed by the IRS, the image of all shelters grew more and
more shadowy. But in recent years the IRS has cracked down
fairly effectively on the more blatant tax shelter frauds. And
lots of dubious write-offs have become illegal. You can still
be stung, and I hear of patently crooked schemes now and
then. But the risks for most people today are of a different
nature.

First there is the expanded IRS campaign on shelters in
general. Because distortions of the law were so common, the
IRS has enlarged its surveillance of tax shelters. If they find
something unacceptable in a limited partnership, they will
disallow some of the benefits to the investors, and if you are
one of those investors, you will owe some back taxes. In actual practice the IRS starts out by auditing the shelter, usually a *private* limited partnership. If they find something
wrong with the deal, they will go after the individuals who
are limited partners in that deal, and they will go back to
their personal returns and disallow some or all write-offs.

Generally speaking, *public* programs in real estate and oil and gas have little trouble with the IRS. Private deals, limited partnerships with forty, thirty-five or fewer participants, get a harder scrutiny and are more likely to be subject to disallowance. These shelters often involve larger write-offs and are the sort that appeal most to high-bracket taxpayers.

The PG risks

Shelters also share the risks of investments that don't offer similar tax benefits. I think real estate shelters, for example, are probably less risky than most others. Still, what happens to the development of townhouses you invest in, that brilliantly conceived and structured deal planned for San Francisco's next gentrified area, when that area totally resists change? Or what if your property thousands of miles away is mismanaged? Or burns down? What happens, in other words, when your investment hits some of the trouble that can befall any real estate project?

Or take oil and gas ventures. Everybody knows that this is a very risky world, or at least one part of it, "exploratory drilling," is. Exploratory drilling takes place in new areas, and even though these days considerable science is applied in deciding where to drill, you might drill ten holes and come up dry. Drill ten more and still no oil.

You still get all your tax write-offs whether you strike oil or not. But what happens to your investment in such a case? Because if you get no return on that $10,000 or $20,000 you invested, you have one lousy deal. Your write-offs are not enough in themselves to justify the investment.

My PG recommendation is to spread your risk. I don't like people to invest in exploratory shelters unless they can afford to buy several of them. You need $30,000 worth of shelter and, for whatever reasonably sound reasons, you want oil? Then let's buy $10,000 worth of one program, $10,000 of another, the same amount of a third.

There is, to be sure, another kind of oil and gas program with much less risk — "developmental drilling." This involves drilling in established fields, where your chances of hitting oil or gas are extremely high. Some of these programs are very consistent. They drill twenty wells and hit oil nineteen times. Your tax benefits here will be the same, but you will not get the kind of return that is possible with exploratory wells that hit big. Some programs are part exploratory, part developmental; they try to give you some assurance of income, plus a shot at a big strike.

Earlier, when I was sketching out the mechanics of a real estate shelter, I'm sure you scratched in the margin: "*Must I invest every year? Supposing I haven't got the $ in 3rd year? Or don't need shelter then?*"

Lots of people have that worry, especially with their first shelter. I've never had a client get into trouble for that reason, but I've never put a client into a real estate deal with multiple payments who didn't have reasonable assurance of earning 50% bracket income for years to come.

Sometimes I find that people who have sudden increases in income have a hard time adjusting to the idea that they have entered the tax shelter realm. Even when their new earnings are real, and not likely to dip or vanish, they have trouble grasping the reality of their new status. That was the case at first with the Mulloys I told you about. Their combined incomes, you may recall, more than doubled in a matter of months, going from $70,000 to $145,000. When I told them we needed a real estate shelter, and quickly, they both got nervous. But I reminded them that it wasn't as though they had just won a horse race. Jan had tripled her salary as a result of that enormous government contract, but her high income would continue. And Mike's salary increase came with his new job. Both of them showed every sign of growing only more and more successful in their fields.

I have certainly heard of cases in which people bought real

estate shelters unwisely and a few years into them couldn't afford them and didn't need them. Not a happy situation, because shelters are not very liquid. You can sell them, often through the broker who sold you the shelter to begin with. But you will take a beating on your sale, and you may be in trouble with the IRS for having taken tax write-offs that will now be subject to "recapture."

"Crossover" is a term I mentioned earlier and an element of some shelters that you must bear in mind. It marks the point at which your tax write-offs run out and your sheltered deal starts to generate income, often "phantom income." "Phantom" means just what the word says, income that you have to declare on your tax return but that does not exist: You don't actually receive any money from the shelter.

If it's a highly leveraged real estate shelter, one that produces very big write-offs, as the crossover period approaches, perhaps ten years after the deal started, your general partner will try to sell the project and give everyone a share of a nice long-term capital gain.

It is possible, of course, that the real estate market is not so good at the time of crossover. Say that the general partner goes to sell, can't get a decent price and has to wait. Make-believe income is recorded, and you have no recourse but to report it and pay tax on it. But nowadays with real estate, it makes sense to sell several years before crossover, and if that is the case, your general partner will have those years to work on the sale before you reach an adverse tax status.

Phantom income is more common and much more important in equipment-leasing deals. These are structured to give you very big write-offs for the first three or four years, perhaps as much as four to one. Then, often in the fifth year, you get a form in the mail that says you have earned $16,432 this year from your leasing tax shelter.

You shake that envelope and peer inside, but no check is to be found. Nor does one come in any subsequent mail. That is phantom income, the result, you might say, of being allowed to defer all those taxes for the first four years. In fact, deferral is the essence of equipment-leasing shelters. But now, according to the IRS, you have earned $16,432 and you'd better declare it on your return.

You'd also better be prepared with a plan for handling the invisible earnings. I have used such shelters with older clients approaching retirement. We bought the equipment-leasing deals before they retired. While they were still fully employed, they enjoyed the heavy write-offs. Phantom income started as they began retirement and their ordinary earnings dropped. Since their bracket had dropped with their earnings, they could simply declare the income and pay taxes on it at a low rate.

I've oversimplified. Suffice it to say that you should only go into equipment leasing with foresight and a plan for handling what's going to happen in the later years of the deal.

Your best route to a shelter

The best and safest approach to a shelter is through your own broker, which might sound a bit self-serving, since I am also a stockbroker, but let me explain.

The brokerage houses that sell shelters have a stake in what they offer. They are, after all, selling to their wealthiest customers, because anyone other than a 50%-bracket person shouldn't and usually doesn't invest in them. No broker wants to lose his best customers by selling them a lemon of a shelter.

Not only that, but the most likely buyer of a tax shelter is someone who has already bought one. A dissatisfied customer will walk away from a second deal.

These brokerage firms maintain special tax shelter departments. They fly people out to the site in Seattle to see the neighborhood where the housing project is to be built. They have their own specialists dissect the impenetrable prospectuses and other documents that describe each deal. They break out all the shelter's numbers and test them for soundness.

What is the stability and true potential of the deal? What is the record of the people who are floating the venture? Have they done other housing projects like this one and with what success? Have they drilled on this site before? How sound are their numbers? How reasonable are their projections?

In my firm it is said that it costs us up to $50,000 to investigate and evaluate some shelters. The number seems high to me, but I do know that our people study a project much more thoroughly than any individual could afford to, and we reject countless deals because we can quickly spot the ones that aren't going to be worth the expense of checking out, a judgment a pro can often make at a glance.

By the time a deal is brought to me to sell to my clients, I can safely assume that it is not a scam and indeed has certain merits. Whether it is juicy enough for my clients or serves their needs is another matter. Our firm offers some forty or fifty real estate deals in a year, another six or seven big oil and gas offerings, maybe one or two small, privately placed oil and gas deals. Of those, I might be interested in only a third after making my own examination and evaluation, and I'm constantly in competition with my colleagues to get my customers into the deals I like the best.

I hear about other shelter projects all the time and have nothing to do with them. Since they haven't been checked out by my firm and I can't do the job myself, I simply can't offer them to my clients with any confidence.

What my firm does and the way I work are what you should be getting from your firm and your broker. If your broker is nothing but a stock jockey, you're in trouble. In fact, you're in trouble if you are looking for a tax shelter or any kind of investment other than stocks.

Brokers of that narrowness aren't going to know when a shelter is good for you, which kind, how much you need. They might pass one along to you, but in all likelihood it's the blind leading the blind. In Chapter 17, we'll consider what you should be looking for in a broker. Breadth of knowledge is terribly important. Whether it's a shelter or an investment in common stocks, much more than a commission should be on your broker's mind.

The commission on a shelter deal is substantial, often around 4% to the broker, plus what his firm makes. Do you have some ongoing relationship with the broker and a confidence that is built over time? Have you been pleased enough with him to send him other customers? The more he needs you, the more he wants to do right by you.

A bit further on in this chapter, we'll see how your accountant and your lawyer can work for you as interpreters and advisers on shelter deals.

They may also be the source of your shelter. Usually it is the large accounting and law firms that offer shelters, and they do it with an approach that is similar to that of a good brokerage firm. They have departments that specialize in shelters, that sift and select and analyze. But be wary of shelters recommended by individual accountants or lawyers.

The question of conflict of interest is often thrown at a lawyer or accountant who is both selling you a shelter and advising you on its merits.

I think it comes down, as it does with the broker who sells you a shelter, to the individual relationship. The accountant or lawyer knows he might place all of your business in jeopardy if he leads you into a bad deal. And you know whether this person understands shelters sufficiently to be making a sound recommendation to you, even if his firm is pushing something. The same goes for Independent Financial Planners. They have an edge because they can team up with any "packager" of shelters they think is good, and unlike brokers, are not limited to the offerings of the head office's tax shelter department.

Doing battle with a prospectus

Once I recommend a shelter, I give my client the prospectus for the offering, urge him to look it over himself and, more importantly, ask to have his accountant or lawyer review it.

A prospectus for a shelter is often an ominous thing, as thick as a phone book and mostly unintelligible to a lay person.

The prospectus is supposed to state every possible fact and condition known or imaginable about the project. Above all, it should make clear to any potential investor what risks are involved and that no promises of success are being made.

That is not unreasonable of lawmakers to require. But in the hands of the lawyers who specialize in shelters, these statements of intention can become parodies and monuments to legal obfuscation.

You can pick out relevant numbers, like the amount you'll be committed to investing and for how many years. And you can read about the general partners who are putting the whole thing together and possibly figure out how much of the money will be going to them.

But only an expert can make enough sense of the whole project as it is buried in the prospectus to render a sound opinion.

One of the most confusing things for the lay person is the practice of statement and counterstatement in a prospectus. You read about the building schedule for a housing project and it seems to be very carefully blocked out. Then you hit a sentence such as, "Construction of the Project entails risks which are beyond the control of the Builder . . ."

Or you think you understand something about the corporate structure of the operation, important to you because your tax benefits are directly tied to that structure. It seems okay until you hit a couple of phrases like these: "Although each Investor Limited Partner (that's you) will receive an opinion of counsel that both the Investor Partnership and the Operating Partnership will be considered partnerships for Federal income tax purposes, that opinion is not binding on the Internal Revenue Service . . ."

Or, "THERE IS NO ASSURANCE THAT THE IRS WILL NOT CHALLENGE CERTAIN CLAIMED DEDUCTIONS . . ."

Or you think that you follow the projections and can see what your write-offs will be and what financial return you can hope to receive on your money. Except, "Future operating results are impossible to predict and no representation or warranty of any kind is made by the operating partnership . . ."

What is happening in plain and capital letters is that the shelter's lawyers are making every conceivable qualification. They promise you, in other words, nothing but potential trouble. And then if there is real trouble they can say, "We told you so."

A tip: Use an expert to translate

So I urge my customers to do whatever reading of the dreaded prospectus they want, but be sure to review it with a competent accountant or lawyer. Not that they should expect a business judgment from one of their professionals. It's quite unlikely that their accountant or lawyer would be willing to say, "Great deal, can't lose." However, they can pass judgment on the technical aspects of the deal. Do the numbers make sense? Are the legal statements, positions sound?

And I give my customers an extra, perhaps gratuitous piece of advice: Be sure and pay the accountant or lawyer a fee for doing the job.

I have found that a number of my clients, especially if

they are new to shelters, don't understand that a real analysis of a prospectus is quite a piece of work. So they toss it at their accountants and casually say, "Could you take a look at this, Dave, give me your opinion?"

Now, if they toss it at their lawyers with the same requests, chances are the lawyers will say, "Sure, remind them that it will probably take many hours to do the job properly and of course they bill by the hour.

Lawyers work that way. Accountants usually don't and I can't tell you why. But the accountant is more likely to say nothing, take the prospectus and then kill the investment. He's not going to put in the time to do the job, since he doesn't know what, if anything, you're prepared to pay him. This is not like doing your tax returns, in which a fee schedule of one kind or another is established.

Further, he sees himself in a no-win situation. Even if he does the analysis, how can he be certain the shelter will work out for you? You could get into trouble with the IRS, and then you'd blame him. The only thing certain, if he gives his approval, is a fat commission to the stockbroker who is selling the deal.

The simple solution for him is to give the prospectus a very quick glance and then mutter something like, "I'm not crazy about their projections." That solves all his problems: No time, no vulnerability.

The fees will vary of course, but I remind my clients that they are considering an investment of, say, $75,000 in a real estate shelter over four to six years. If they can get thorough appraisals from accountants or lawyers and it costs $1000 or so, that is hardly a stiff price for insurance. But bear in mind that this sort of thing is *not* needed for a public program; there, a less detailed examination will do.

Sometimes the special complications of shelters make a potential investor mistrust them to the point where he won't invest. One investor I had like that was Carl Katz, a fellow who prided himself on a knowledge of finance. He had survived three separate dress companies on Seventh Avenue and was running a fourth one with considerable success when I first recommended a shelter to him.

It was an extremely good real estate deal, a thing of the past. A "Section 8," it was called, a form of housing development with heavy government rent subsidy. Under this one, apartments were to be built in a suburb of Memphis, in a market where rents would normally be nearly $500. With the government paying a chunk of the rent, however, the tenants would have to pay only something like $250. Anytime you've got apartments worth $500 and you're giving them away for $250, you don't have to worry much about vacancies.

The deal would give Katz slightly better than two to one in write-offs. The first year he'd invest $14,000 and be able to write off $30,000 in taxes. Over six years he'd put in $70,000, for which, over the lifetime of the project, he'd receive tax losses of $190,000. In his 50% bracket, that would amount to $95,000 going into his pocket instead of to the federal government, plus additional savings on state taxes.

A terrific deal and, as I said, a thing of the past. Section 8 projects were last offered in 1983. The Reagan administration was against that sort of government support for housing.

When I called Katz to offer him a chance to invest in this shelter, it was several weeks after he and I had first agreed that he would need one and that I would keep my eyes open for him. I was quite pleased with myself, assuming that someone as knowledgeable in money matters as Carl would fully appreciate this opportunity and that we could get him in it quickly.

"Okay," he said when I called him and described the shelter to him, "send me the prospectus and I'll look it over."

"Good, and be sure and have Martin review it too." I knew his accountant and thought this offering would make great sense to him.

"Martin? What do I need Martin for?"

"You know a lot about finance, Carl," I said to him. "But you've never owned a shelter before. They're not like other investments, and I really think you should have Martin look over the prospectus too. And pay him a fee."

"What's wrong with you, Stanley? If you recommend a stock to me, we talk about it, I read about it and then decide. You think I run to Martin every time I buy a stock from you?"

"Well, okay," I replied. "Do as you please. I'll send you the prospectus."

I didn't hear from Katz for about a week, and when I called him he was uncharacteristically vague. He was still reviewing the prospectus.

Offerings are made, and when they have the prescribed number of investors, that's it. Good deals, naturally, go rather quickly, in three to four weeks.

Katz called back after this Section 8 had closed. Fortunately, he didn't want to invest, even if he had the wrong reasons for his decision.

"I never invest in anything I can't understand, Stanley," he told me. "I never read anything with more double-talk in my life."

"Carl, I've got sad news for you. That is the nature of the beast. Every prospectus for a private offering I have ever looked at is the same."

"So how can you, a reasonably sound man, invest in the things? Or worse, recommend them to me?"

"That's why I wanted you to show it to Martin," I told him. "He's a professional in these things, and he'd be able to make sense of it."

"What you're telling me, Stanley, is that even though I can't understand what the hell they're talking about, I should trust you and Martin."

"I suppose so," I replied.

"With all due respect, Stanley, that makes me uncomfortable."

"Carl, you feel that way, then don't do it. There is no law that says you've got to invest in a tax shelter."

"Yeah, but there *is* a goddamn law that says if I don't, I've got to give all that money to the government."

It took a year, but Carl finally made the plunge. Martin and I have now put him into several shelters, more than one a year, which he needed because of his high income. I would estimate that he has saved himself about $200,000 that would otherwise have gone in taxes.

Even if you have your Martin review the deal, there are several questions you should discuss with your broker.

What are the track record and background of the promoters? Of the general partners? Who are all the central figures?

How long have they been in this business? How many deals like this have they done? Has any ever blown up on them? Have they ever had any legal trouble related to their shelter business?

What are the ages and backgrounds and years of experience of the principal employees of the general partners? Has the head been in the building business (assuming this is a real estate shelter) for fifteen years? And do, his senior people have, say, some eighty years' experience among them?

Is this the same kind of real estate project these people have been connected with before? If this is a residential project, have they been doing these or been in shopping centers?

How many projects has your brokerage firm done with these people?

What future projects do you know they have in development? (With other projects planned, they'll have that much more incentive to make this one successful.)

How much are the promoters and the general partners investing themselves?

82

Checklist for Chapter 6

1. Shelters are not the magic way to cut down on your taxes. They are, in fact, only to be considered after you have invested in all of the various tax-advantaged vehicles that are available to you; after you have converted taxable interest income into tax-free; after you have done everything possible with retirement plans.

2. The most likely candidate for a tax shelter is someone who earns upward of $150,000 in salaried income. If you pay more than $30,000 in federal income tax, you surely ought to consider a tax shelter. If you pay $20,000 to $25,000, you're a possible candidate for a tax shelter. If you've had a large short-term capital gain, you might want to buy a shelter.

3. The biggest write-off won't produce the biggest income and the biggest capital gain. Tax shelter investing involves a compromise between various kinds of economic advantages. You've got to evaluate the total benefit of the shelter to you. You should never buy a shelter just for the sake of a write-off.

4. Tax shelter investments carry all of the risks of ordinary investments and more. They can fail economically — your oil well may not produce any oil — or they can be challenged by the IRS and have some of their write-offs disallowed.

5. The best way to find and invest in a shelter is through your stockbroker, assuming that he is more than just a pusher of stocks, or through a reliable financial planner. Have your accountant or lawyer review the shelter, and expect to pay him for his time and brains.

CHAPTER 7

Your home as an investment

ONE OF MY FAVORITE clients was a Washington editor, a man of great humor and energy who was essentially fearless when it came to money.

Whenever I went to Washington, I always stopped by his office, not only because I had business to review with him, but because I got a kick out of his big city room. As I walked through, images from every newspaper movie ever made raced through my mind, and I always expected someone to shout, "Stop the presses!"

His office was called "the fishbowl." It had a large glass window which looked on the whole city room and which permitted everyone on the staff to peer in, see who was with the boss and how the conversation seemed to be going.

Sitting in there one afternoon, my friend, whom I'll call Benton, pointed to the distant corner of the city room. "I got a real estate editor out there, Stanley, can't tell me where the local real estate market is going to be a year from now."

"Not such an easy thing to do."

"That's what you say. I say that's his job. What good is the guy, can't tell me where things will be in a year?"

"I didn't know you were in the market."

"I'm always in the real estate market."

In fact, he had probably owned more homes than anyone I ever knew. As part of his career, he had been a foreign correspondent for a couple of magazines, and wherever he was based he bought a home. Never rented.

"With those homes you've owned all over the world, you ever get burned?"

"Never," he said. "I sometimes couldn't get my money out exactly when I wanted. Kay and I would have to move to another country by a certain date, and we simply couldn't unload the house by then. But even then it never took very long to sell, and I always made money."

"Are you actually looking for a new place now?" I asked. They had bought a massive Victorian house in Georgetown only two years before and, so far as I knew, really liked the big old place.

"Well, we are, we aren't. I heard of something good Kay's going to take a look at. But we're not really looking."

We went on to other matters, and about twenty minutes later he took a phone call. "We got a new house?" he fairly shouted into the phone. "Fantastic, fantastic. Yeah, yeah, yeah, I'll meet you out there at six-thirty. You're right, I'd better take a real look at the place before I buy it."

Obviously my friend Benton was not the average house buyer. And though his style might have been a bit too cavalier, there is a lot in his approach to buying homes I can recommend.

Unfortunately most people approach such a move under a large dark cloud. "Can I make the payments?" they ask. "What happens if I can't or don't? How much can I afford, anyway? Where can I get the down payment?"

My answer to all of these questions and fears is, "Do it." And once I explain to clients the financial and tax benefits involved in owning their home rather than renting a place, they are able to make the largest investment of their lives with confidence.

Not long ago I got a call full of home-buying questions from Howard Zale, the son of one of my longtime clients. After five years of marriage, Howard and his wife, Rachel, were now expecting their first child. Until this time they had been renting a house in southern New Jersey, not feeling any need to own a place. A child changes that feeling in an almost biologic way.

With the baby due in seven months, they had begun to look around and Howard wanted guidance. "I think we're spinning our wheels," he said. "It appears that the kind of house we'd like in today's market will cost us $150,000. But that seems to me like a staggering amount of money. Also, I hear all kinds of advice. One person says we should not spend more than twice what we earn in a year. Another person says the payments and expenses we have on the house should not be more than a quarter of what we earn. Straighten me out, Stanley. What can we afford, if anything?"

Howard earned $40,000 a year as a high-level administrator for a large university. If he performed the same tasks in the business world, he'd more than double his salary. But he liked academia, wasn't about to change that. Rachel earned about $35,000 a year in a public-opinion research organization. Howard told me that she expected to take a six-month leave when the baby was born, so they'd be without her income for that stretch of time.

The first thing I told him was to forget all those supposed guidelines, like spending no more than a quarter of their income. "All of those things were conceived of years ago at a time when prices were much lower, when it was very rare to have two incomes in a family and when taxes were so low, you didn't even think of them in your calculations. Also, that kind of thinking doesn't take into account what your tax benefits are going to be in today's world. Without figuring those into the whole picture, you simply can't know what a house will really cost you."

"That may be," he replied, "but if those rules don't apply anymore, there must be others that do. I mean, I don't really know if we can afford a $150,000 house or not."

"Forget the figure $150,000," I told him.

"How can I forget it, Stanley? That's what I'm looking at if we buy this house. And by the way, it's a nice house."

"I mean forget it because in the real world you aren't going to have to worry about the whole sum of $150,000. What you have to concern yourself with is, first, the amount of cash you'll need for the down payment on the house. How much and where will you get it? And how much interest will you have to pay for that money? Then you have to focus on the interest you'll have to pay the bank for the mortgage. In other words, what is going to be the interest cost on all the money you'll have to borrow, and will you be able to handle that?"

"Is it legal to borrow both the down payment and the mortgage?"

"The law has nothing to do with it. The only consideration is whether you can cover the interest payments you'll owe the bank and anyone else you might borrow from."

He told me that the best mortgage deal he had found required him to put down 25% of the purchase price of the house, or $37,500. The bank would lend him the balance of $112,000 and charge him 13% interest, a fixed rate for thirty years.

"Fine. Have you got $37,500?" I asked.

"Nothing like it," he said. "You know Rachel and I both have been putting $2000 a year for the last few years into our IRAs. We could start there. Draw that money out."

"Terrible idea," I told him. "You'd get murdered with taxes plus penalties for early withdrawals."

"So what do we do? Forget the house and just go on renting?"

"No, no. Renting is always a bad idea. Let's just review a few possibilities. I think I know where we can find this money."

Being familiar with his circumstances, I first considered his retirement plan.

"I thought you said we couldn't touch our IRAs."

"I'm not talking about that. I'm talking about the plan you've been contributing to at the university. The law does permit you to borrow from that."

As it turned out, he could borrow about $13,000 from the fund and have to pay only 4% interest on it. We'd already come up with nearly a third of the down payment.

He and Rachel owned a small amount of stock. The house was a good reason to sell it. That was $6000 more.

They had some cash in a money market account and felt they could pull $5000 from those savings. We were up to $24,000.

For the balance of $13,500, I advised him to do what so many young people do to buy their first home — ask their parents for help. His father, I knew well, could afford an interest-free loan of that amount and in fact was delighted to lend him the money.

So, quite painlessly, we had assembled the down payment of $37,500, and of that, in terms of immediate payments and cash flow, all they would have to think about was 4% interest owed on the $13,000 borrowed from the retirement fund. That amounted to $43.33 a month.

Beyond that, of course, was the monthly payment to the bank of $1238.95.

I told Howard that there were two ways to look at that amount: cash flow and aftertaxes.

He and Rachel were going to have to come up with that $1282.28 each month, and that was a lot of money for them. Still, they were presently paying $800 rent. So we were talking about not quite $500 more, plus maintenance costs.

"You take a vacation last year?" I asked him.

"Europe. Three weeks. It was heaven."

"You know what it cost you?"

"Not exactly, but I'd hate to give up our vacations."

"Supposing I told you that for the two of you, a vacation

in Europe for three weeks must have cost you at least $6000. And the difference between what you're now paying in rent and what you'd be paying on those loans would be $6000 a year."

"It still hurts. You don't know what our vacations mean to us."

"Think of it this way: Maybe you don't go to Europe for a year or two or three. That's not the end of the world. And think about what you're getting instead."

"It still hurts."

"Okay, then maybe we see what the tax advantages are, and you'll be able to figure a way to own your house and still go to Europe after the first year."

"That sounds better, much better."

The tax law allows him as a home owner to deduct from his taxes all the interest he pays on his mortgage, plus his real estate taxes.

Each monthly payment to the bank is divided between the interest on their loan and paying off the principal of the loan. On a thirty-year loan, only a tiny part of the payment would go toward the principal in the first few years. In fact, of the $15,387.36 that he and Rachel would pay, nearly $15,000 would be interest in the first year. They could deduct that from their taxes, and it meant, in their 42% bracket, that they would be saving about $6000. "That's enough to take you back to Europe," I told him, "and you're also owning the home — a great asset that we can assume is going to be increasing in value."

Further, his real estate taxes for that town in New Jersey would be about $1700 a year. Every penny of it would also be deductible from their income taxes.

"Do it," I told him firmly. "You'd be absolutely crazy not to. And don't lose sleep over it, either. You can make those interest payments, and that's all you have to be concerned with. The best deal of your life."

"I have to admit, Stanley, you do make it sound good. But

I have one last question: Should we wait until the interest rates drop? Everybody says they're going to go even lower. We might save a lot of money."

The question of a still-frightened fellow. "Don't wait. You and Rachel need a home, and as we just saw, you can afford the one you want. Say you find in a few years that the interest rates on mortgages have dropped two points or more, of which there is hardly any guarantee. Then you can always get yourself a new mortgage and pay off the old one. Either from your own bank, because they won't want to lose you as a customer, or from another bank across the street competing with them. Either way it would cost you some money, but you'd get a new mortgage at the lower rate, and you wouldn't have lost the house you want or the benefits we talked about by owning."

"Stanley, I think you're right," he said. "It's still a big step."

"Do it," I said once again. And I'm happy to say, they did.

The great buy versus rent debate

The tax benefits I reviewed with Howard apply only if you own a home. If you rent, you get none of them. Your landlord does.

Even so, I get people from time to time giving me the argument that it really is better to rent than to buy. "Look at all the money I'll have to invest," they say, as if everyone were J.P. Morgan.

They are so wrong. Let's take the figures we just used for Howard and Rachel to see what really happens.

Let's say that they took the $37,500 cash we pulled together for the down payment and invested it aggressively in the stock market. And let's assume that all of their investments are long-term capital gains, so their taxes are not too stiff on their gains.

Well, in that sense we can look at the house as a long-term

capital gain instrument, but one on whose profit you don't have to pay taxes for a long, long time, if ever. As the value of the house grows, those profits just sit there.

When you finally sell your house, if you do, then you would have to pay long-term capital gains taxes, but with some wonderfully favorable twists, such as having the first $125,000 of your profit completely tax-free if you're fifty-five or older when you sell. If you're an aggressive trader in the stock market, chances are you're going to be buying and selling as soon as a year and a day has passed, if you can wait even that long, and so you'll be paying taxes over and over again.

No leverage like real estate leverage

Then there's the whole business of "leverage." Leverage is when you buy something with a small amount of your money and a large loan of someone else's money.

In the case of real estate, you have the best leveraged investment I know. You put down 20% to 30% of the total cost of the house and the bank lends you the other 70% or 80%. As we saw, Howard and Rachel had to come up with $37,500 and they were titled owners of a house worth $150,000.

In the stock market, you can get a certain amount of leverage from your broker. He is your banker, as it were, and on a margin account he will lend you up to 50% of your purchase. So if Howard and Rachel used their $37,500 in cash for stocks, they could actually be owners of $75,000 worth of stock.

But that is nothing compared with what they can get in real estate. There the $37,500 brings them value of $150,000. Whereas in the stock market the leveraged value is only $75,000.

We can't really make a direct comparison of profit here because we don't know what stocks are going to be bought or what will actually happen to the value of a given house.

It's conceivable that a skillful investor could increase the value of his holdings so that it would rise as much as the value of a home, maybe more. But generally his risk would be considerably greater. And generally that investor would have to be extremely skillful and lucky.

Also, no matter how skillful and lucky he is, I doubt that he'll be able to live in his flashy investments. In the rent versus buy argument, strangely, folks forget this. When you buy, you are living in your investment. And if you're like most people, you're getting pleasure from your investment.

In the end there are those tax advantages. All of the write-offs from the interest on the mortgage and the real estate taxes belong to home owners only. The stock market investor gets none of that, although if he has a margin account he may deduct the interest on that. Still, the difference is great and the chance of loss is great.

As a financial planner, I have yet another reason for wanting my clients to own their homes. I spoke earlier of diversification of assets. One way to create it is to spread your investments in the stock market among several different kinds of stocks. That helps, but I'm not fully comfortable if you have everything in paper. I want to see some "hard assets," and real estate is the pre-eminent hard asset.

Now, it is true that a hard asset like a home cannot be sold with the ease of a stock. But if you have balance in your investments, one of the things you have is a source of cash. You might not be able to sell your house quickly or you might not want to sell in a depressed market, even though you might have a sudden need for cash. But we're going to have things planned so that you will be able to sell some stocks, or bonds perhaps, to provide you cash instead.

Buy, do not rent, I tell my clients.

CHAPTER 8

Taking profits out of your home

ONE OF THE BEST sources of cash is one of the least used. It's your home.

Over and over I've heard people say that even though the value of their home has gone up and up, it's all a paper gain, of no use to them in the real world.

"What good does it do me?" they say. "If I sell the place to get my profit out, then I'm faced with buying another house. And unless I plan on moving to another, depressed part of the world, I'm going to have to spend all I get from my house, and probably more, to buy another one. So while it makes me feel good to know that I bought well and wisely some years ago and I'm living in a small gold mine, in fact I can't put my hands on the gold. I don't intend to move to Pakistan."

In fact that's all wrong. You can put your hands on that gold and you can increase its value.

Doing so is a technique I frequently use in devising plans, especially for people who have little cash available. Without cash, it's very tough for us to develop assets. We have nothing to invest with.

The Berelsons were in that situation when they came to me to figure out a way they could retire in seven years, when he reached sixty-two. He wanted early retirement, he told me quite frankly, because he didn't like his job any more and had never much liked the people he worked for. Sad to say, he had been with them for about twenty-five years.

I am not a psychiatrist, but it became clear to me as we got into their situation that Berelson was a rigid man, beset by a variety of fears. Though he had been unhappy with his work for years, he had been afraid to leave and try something new. And his fears rendered him an extremely conservative investor.

Relatively speaking, in his job he had not done badly. At fifty-four, he was earning $65,000 a year as a vice-president of a medium-sized company that manufactured industrial hardware. It was a very old-fashioned company, family owned and dominated, and it was a family that believed in noblesse oblige rather than contemporary employee-management practices, always a much less costly way of running a business. They maintained a Christmas bonus plan, right out of Dickens: Sam Berelson, after all his years and his position, received a warm $50 as well as, of course, a frozen turkey, which was handed out to each employee. Consistent with this nineteenth-century approach to labor, the company offered no retirement plan, which is rare these days, but which I encounter now and then.

It was a sad and serious deficiency for the Berelsons. They felt somewhat trapped, wanting to get out of that company in a mere seven years, but with little to retire on. Mrs. Nina Berelson was a speech therapist earning about $25,000, and she had only a small retirement fund built over recent years.

They had no current cash problems, earning $90,000 together and living rather modestly. Their only child, a daughter, was going through college on a partial scholarship, so not much drain there. About their only act of indulgence, if it could be called that, was a two-week winter holiday in Sarasota, Florida, where Sam's sister lived. They liked Sarasota so much that they wanted to retire there somehow and, if possible, buy a condominium to live in there.

I thought I saw a glimmer of light when Sam handed me a manila folder with "STOCKS AND BONDS" neatly typed across the top. "Here's a rundown of all the investments I've made over the years," he said.

When I opened the folder, the light faded. Sam was neat and orderly and hopelessly conservative. There was Goodyear, which he'd bought in 1971 at $34 a share, and twelve years later, when we were reviewing his affairs, it was selling at about 30. He had American Can, bought in 1968 at 55, now down to 45. Eastman Kodak was another of his blue-chip specials: bought in 1972 at $140 a share, today worth about 70. U.S. Steel he bought in 1964 at 64. Indeed he told me he thought he had a real bargain with that one because it had been selling for more than 100 four or five years earlier. It split three for two in 1976, his records showed, but even so, adjusting for the split, he had a big loss, with the stock selling around 27. DuPont, the wondrous duPont, he paid $175 a share for in 1973, enjoyed a three-for-one split along the way, yet he still showed a loss with the stock now going for 51.

You'll get a better sense of how painful it was for me to review this list when we consider, in Chapters 10 and 11, what I think is the smart way to invest in the market, part of which has to do with selecting growth stocks, not household names with as much chance at growth as the dinosaurs.

Fortunately, not all of his stocks were distinguished losers. But still, it was a dismal portfolio and it represented about half of all his investments. The rest were bonds, not surprisingly, which were down in price and also taxable.

What we had to do was obvious. "Mr. Berelson, we have more talking and exploring to do, but at this point it's pretty clear we should sell a good part of your portfolio, take the tax losses and reinvest that money so we can get some growth from stocks and tax-free income from bonds."

"Reinvest in what?" he asked.

"I can't give you a list at the moment. But we're talking about real growth stocks."

"You mean computers?" he said, his voice rising.

"Well, computers, health services, communications systems, any number of areas that are growing, that are the future of the economy, not the past."

"Too risky for me, Mr. Cohen, much too risky for me."

"Mr. Cohen, you may mean well," Mrs. Berelson said, "but obviously you don't understand us. We're conservative people, Mr. Cohen, in everything we do. In the way we lead our lives, in our politics and certainly in how we handle our money."

"I can see that, Mrs. Berelson."

"Then why in the world are you even suggesting that we take all the money we have and gamble it on one of those here-today-gone-tomorrow computer companies?"

I thought for a moment she was going to cry.

"Why don't you tell us to go to Las Vegas and bet on black?" she added.

Mr. Berelson covered her hand with his. "Easy, Nina, easy. There are all kinds of computer companies."

"I won't hear of it, Sam. My God, you wouldn't sleep a single night if you owned that kind of stock."

"Look, Mrs. Berelson, Mr. Berelson, I think perhaps you're getting worked up over nothing," I told them. "I'm not going to try to convince you to invest in something you can't live with. If computers and growth stocks in general give you sleepless nights, we'll find another way of doing this."

"Like what?" she asked sharply.

"Like something with less risk," I replied, trying to keep my voice even. "Let me ask you a few questions about your home."

It was a guess, but an informed one. As I suspected, they had practically no mortgage on their house. They had bought it for $30,000 a number of years ago, and their mortgage was now down to around $7000. They lived in Massachusetts, not far from the New Hampshire border, an area that has boomed in land values in recent years. Berelson thought his house was worth about $150,000 in today's market.

"That's where we can get the capital we need to build your retirement fund," I told them. "Take out a new mortgage."

Mrs. Berelson looked at me as if I had really lost my mind. "A new mortgage, Mr. Cohen? Good Lord, don't you realize we're close to paying off the one we have now?"

"I do, Mrs. Berelson, I do indeed. Just let me show you how we can do this. Think of your home as an investment you made years ago, a very wise investment, where your money has multiplied many times. Now we want to pull some of that profit out."

The bank, I explained, would lend them about three-quarters of the value of the house, less the balance of their present mortgage. And the bank would undervalue the house, we could be sure. So if Mr. Berelson figured their home was worth about $150,000, the bank would send their appraiser out and he would come up with, say, $115,000.

That meant that after $7000 had been used to pay off the old mortgage and a few thousand more went for points the bank charges, their new mortgage loan would be around $75,000.

"In short," I told them happily, "the bank gives you a new mortgage, which means you get a check for $75,000 that you can do anything you want with."

"And what would you have us do with it, Mr. Cohen?" Mrs. Berelson asked. "Buy some hot stock? Or just take a nice cruise around the world . . . I mean, this is absolute madness, Sam. First he wants to load us up with the debt of a whole new mortgage, then he wants us to be some high flyers in the market. I mean, excuse me, Mr. Cohen, but I think you're absolutely cuckoo."

"In fairness, Nina," Mr. Berelson said, "give him a chance. I really don't think he has hot stocks in mind, after what we've discussed. Mr. Cohen, what do you have in mind?"

"I'd take the $75,000, or a portion, and put it in a safe investment that would grow in value over the next seven years and which would fit directly into your retirement plans."

"And what is that?"

"A condominium in Sarasota, Florida."

They looked at each other, and I thought I noticed a change in the light in Mrs. Berelson's eyes.

"Tell us more," she said.

"You told me you want to retire in Sarasota. These days, the condo market down there is depressed. So you could probably get yourselves a good buy. The down payment comes out of your $75,000. For the next seven years, you rent out the condo. The rental market, as opposed to the selling market, is not bad. You should get a pretty good rental, which would cover any mortgage costs on the condo. At the end of seven years, we can be reasonably sure that the value of that condo will have increased, and you then move into it yourselves. You retire and sell your home in Massachusetts, which by that time we can be reasonably sure will also have appreciated in value. And you won't have to pay any taxes on the first $125,000 of your profit because you'll be over age fifty-five by then and be entitled to that exclusion. Furthermore, during those seven years, you'll have the handsome deductions from your taxes for the interest on both mortgages and the real estate taxes on both houses."

"Of course, we'll have to be carrying both those mortgages," Mr. Berelson said.

"Yes, but your Sarasota mortgage should be covered by your rental income. And while your Massachusetts mortgage is going to mean higher payments than you're now making, I can tell you, even before working out the exact numbers, that you and Mrs. Berelson can easily handle that additional expense. In fact, if worst came to worst, you could even handle the mortgage payments in Sarasota if you couldn't rent it out."

Berelson shook his head. "It's unlikely that we wouldn't be able to rent it. I know a bit about that market."

"And as a bonus, part of your vacations in Sarasota will be deductible, since part of the time you're down there you'll be looking after your rental property. In fact, since that condo will be a business venture, for the next seven years you can deduct everything that goes with the business, things like depreciation, maintenance, insurance."

"I have to admit, Mr. Cohen, that plan sounds much more suitable to us than the other things you suggested," Mrs. Berelson said.

"Thank you."

"But I wonder if I could ask you about two other possibilities."

"Anything."

She reached into her pocketbook and pulled out a small brown spiral notebook. "What about . . ." She flipped a few pages. "What about a single-premium whole life insurance policy or a single-premium deferred annuity?"

I had to smile. "May I ask, Mrs. Berelson, where you came up with those?"

"A friend," she replied. "He said they were good for retirement plans."

"Your friend is right, except in your case. If you took the $75,000 from your new mortgage and bought either the single-premium whole life or the single-premium deferred annuity, you would be inviting a visit from the IRS."

Mr. Berelson looked scornfully at his wife. "Her brother knows everything, Mr. Cohen."

"He didn't say anything about trouble with the IRS to me," she said.

"Depends how you do it," I said, and explained. Both those instruments, as we'll see in Chapter 16 when we examine retirement more fully, are certainly useful in retirement plans.

With both, you take a chunk of money, in the Berelsons' case $75,000, and buy the policy or the annuity. You are paid a set rate of interest, and your money compounds year after year. All of your interest income is tax-deferred. When you retire you have access to the single-premium life money, and you can draw the annuity money in any of a great variety of ways to suit your needs. Depending on the years your money is compounding and the interest rates you're realizing, you have a chance with such a plan to build quite a substantial treasury. In seven years, if the Berelsons received 10% a year, their $75,000 would balloon up to more than $146,000. And all of this with very little risk.

I have oversimplified, but so far as Mrs. Berelson's brother was concerned, that's what he had in mind for them.

The only problem with doing it was the source of their money. They were getting their $75,000 from a new mortgage. They would receive tax deductions on all of the interest they paid to the bank on that mortgage. If they took the $75,000 and bought either the single-premium life or the annuity, they would receive even further tax benefits, the tax-deferred treatment of all their earnings. Alas, Section 264(a)2 of the Internal Revenue Code specifically says you may not do that.

The reality is that people do it and take their chances that the IRS won't find out. But if they are audited and the IRS agent sees a direct correlation between the date of their mortgage and the date they bought that annuity, they're in trouble.

For the same reasons, the IRS won't allow you to refinance your home and take the newfound money and buy tax-free bonds.

But otherwise, neither the IRS nor the bank cares what

you do with that money. You can invest it in common stocks if you want. Or sink it into your own business, or use it to start a business. My clients have used this money in any number of ways.

When Dr. Irwin Parker, Jr., finished his residency and established a medical practice in Springfield, Massachusetts, his parents remortgaged their home and used the money to equip Irwin's office. A noble sacrifice? Not really. Irwin Parker, Sr., is a successful cotton broker in Boston. He phoned me to discuss the mortgage strategy and I was all for it. He wanted to help his son get started, and for him, taking out that mortgage was "creative financing."

Another client of mine, an optometrist who had two offices in Queens, New York, came upon an opportunity to buy out three other offices when their owner died suddenly of a heart attack. My client could have financed the purchase by various means, but when we talked the whole thing over, a new mortgage on his house in Roslyn was clearly the best way to raise the capital.

When Hans Musil and his wife came to me for a financial plan, one of their concerns was that they didn't have the money to buy a summer home they very much wanted. They were tired of paying big summer rentals to other people, but they didn't have the cash for the down payment on the house they had found. I pointed out that their own home in Evanston, Illinois, was worth nearly four times what they had paid for it and that the mortgage was down to a negligible amount. When I suggested that they mortgage one house to buy another, they were somewhat startled. But as the overall financial plan developed, it became apparent to them that it was the right move. They took out a $95,000 mortgage on their house, put part of it into the down payment on the summer home and had money left over to make gifts to their two children.

So if this applies to you, take the bank's money and make

more money with it, even as you're paying off your new mortgage and creating substantial tax write-offs.

That, by the way, is what the Berelsons finally did. They refinanced their Massachusetts home and bought a condo in Sarasota, and though there are still a few years for my scenario to play out, to date things are working wonderfully. They had no trouble renting the condo, and so far as their taxes are concerned, they have found a tax shelter without actually buying one: Their tax deductions and write-offs each year have been truly significant. And, I am delighted to report, I have been able to persuade the Berelsons to invest their sheltered dollars in stocks that both can live with.

When they do retire to Sarasota, they will have a beefed-up portfolio, their social security income, their IRAs, her small pension and what will certainly be a substantial amount of money from the sale of their Massachusetts home. They'll be in good shape, and what's more, they know it. Sam Berelson has relaxed noticeably, and Mrs. Berelson wrote me one of the nicest thank you notes I've ever seen.

CHAPTER 9

The joys of debt

THE RESPONSE of Diane Picker to my best piece of advice was shock.

"Go to the bank and borrow $20,000," I told her.

She squirmed a bit in her chair and stared at me. "Mr. Cohen," she finally said, "I came to you for planning. That's not planning, that's debt. What do I want to be in debt for?"

"So we can do some planning," I replied.

"Mr. Cohen, do not make fun of me."

I apologized for the way it sounded and tried to explain. Quite simply, she was a woman who had no financial assets, and though she was now earning $55,000, I had nothing to work with. To make money — and that was the first part of my modest plan for her — I needed some money.

Diane's situation is fairly common among women. She had been working in advertising for fifteen years, and her salary had crawled up to $30,000. Women's lib changed all that, she told me. "I'm still not paid what men in my same job earn. But I have gone from $30,000 to $55,000 in three years, and I'll go higher, too."

Single, not extravagant, she nevertheless had nothing invested and only a few thousand in a money market fund. She had been married briefly to a failed writer who drank too much. There was never a question of alimony from him, and in fact, from time to time she lent him money, which she never expected to see again and didn't. She told me she didn't expect to marry again, either, but even if she did, she planned to continue working forever. She felt strongly about paying her own way, as she put it, yet she felt a little vulnerable at her age, forty-four, with nobody and nothing financial to fall back on.

Our choice seemed clear. If we waited for her to earn more and so produce the cash we needed to start building some assets, we'd be waiting for years. With a loan from the bank, we could get started immediately. She could use debt to spring herself upward.

I also told her that inflation benefits the borrower. You borrow $1 today, and three years from now you're paying back at an adjusted rate of 80¢. As inflation increases, the value of the dollar goes down. Unfortunately, I don't see inflation disappearing.

"If I were to go into hock for $20,000," she said, "and I must confess the idea of it is rather scary to me — but if I were, what would you do with the money?"

"What scares you? That you couldn't pay it off?"

She paused. "That, I suppose, and the very idea of deliberately throwing myself into debt. I don't know exactly where I got the idea, but I have always lived as free of debt as possible. I don't think of it especially as a sexist thing, although maybe it is. Deep down, I kind of thought that as a woman I had to be especially careful. Like they could fire me at any time, and it'd be tougher for me to stay afloat if I had a lot of debt."

"I recommend debt to many people, and both men and women are often stunned by it," I told her. "They think of debt as something that is wrong, something evil. They seem to get the idea all ensnared with extravagance and reckless spending. But I'm not talking about borrowing $20,000 so you can buy yourself a fast Italian sports car. I'm not talking about self-indulgence at all. I'm talking about self-preservation."

"But $20,000 is still an awful lot of money. At least to me it is. Big rock on my back."

"Forget the total amount," I told her. "Look at the monthly payments. Can you handle that?" Just as I did with young Howard Zale and his potential mortgage, I led Diane through the numbers. We figured that she'd have to pay about $700 a month for three years on her bank loan. She'd have an interest deduction of about $5000. That would reduce her taxes and she could cut her withholding to free up more cash for her monthly payments. She could certainly handle such a loan.

She nodded several times, staring at the figures I had scratched out. "Okay, Mr. Cohen, you make it look possible. Now, what about my other question? What would you do with my $20,000 if I got it for you?"

"Think I'd put the whole nut into an aggressive growth mutual fund, like Oppenheimer Directors, Putnam Vista or Lord Abbott Developing Growth."

"That's it?" she asked. "That's all I'd get for my grief?"

I was puzzled. "What's wrong with a sharp mutual fund?"

"Well, nothing," she replied. "But I kind of expected a little fireworks. You know, $5000 here, $5000 there. Some stocks. Futures. Puts and calls."

I couldn't believe my ears. "Futures? Puts and calls?"

She smiled. "Relax, Mr. Cohen. Just thought I'd tease you a little," she said. "But I did think there'd be more to this so-called plan than one pop at a mutual fund."

I had to admire her style. "Well, the sad fact is that $20,-000 isn't an enormous pile to work with. But there are a couple of other things we could do. Somewhere we'll find another $2000 and get you started with an IRA. And before long we'll have some income and I'll start buying some tax-exempt bonds for you. Your portfolio will start to grow, and so will your net worth."

"What could I earn from your mutual fund?"

"I'd expect to see your money increase at least 30% a year."

"So my $20,000 would become $26,000, $27,000?"

I nodded.

"What happens if you pick the wrong fund?"

"And it doesn't make that much?"

"Supposing it doesn't make anything at all? Supposing the market goes into a tailspin and we lose money? Then what?"

"Well," I said, shrugging, "easy come, easy go."

She gasped.

"Relax," I said, smiling. "My turn to tease you."

"Not funny," she said. "I'd die if I invested $20,000 — a borrowed $20,000 at that — and saw it disappear."

"I do not expect that to happen. But obviously when you invest, you have that risk. Even with a mutual fund, where your chances of losing the whole $20,000 are pretty slight."

"But just suppose it happened, Mr. Cohen. Imagine the worst. What in the world would I do?" she asked, visibly worried. "I'm out $20,000 and I still have to pay off the bank."

"It's not a happy picture, but if you were in that situation, you could handle it."

"I know I could handle it, Mr. Cohen."

"I mean *financially* you could handle it," I told her. "The point I think you're overlooking is that on the basis of what you're earning now and what we can anticipate you'll be earning, you can handle the payments to the bank. Those payments don't get any bigger if you lose your $20,000. You can handle the payments from your current income. Otherwise I wouldn't suggest you borrow the money."

"I suppose you're right," she said reluctantly.

Two good things happened. Diane got a bonus that came to $5000 after taxes, and she trusted me enough to take a bank loan. With the bonus, she cut her loan to $15,000, but we still had a total of $20,000 for the mutual fund.

I knew the fund was good. As it turned out, the market was even better than I had expected. In the course of her first year, she made 40% on her investment, and after another sixteen months, her $20,000 had become $40,000. All long-term gain, too.

Dealing with the happy problem of sudden fame

Derek Conran came to me with a problem that was similar at its core to Diane's: a suddenly inflated level of earning and living that was likely to improve, and no cash.

He was a photographer, only twenty-seven, who had been working around San Francisco. The most he ever earned out there was $25,000, and then he made the big move to New York and he got very lucky. In less than three years, he was "discovered," getting assignments from *Vogue, Town and Country, Esquire.* His income had leaped to $130,000, and that was merely the beginning. Those magazines didn't pay all that well, even though he was hardly complaining. They were establishing him as a photographer for big ad campaigns, where the really big money was made.

Since all of this success and fame had occurred so quickly, Derek had nothing saved or invested. Although he maintained that he was quite ignorant when it came to handling money, his instincts certainly were good. "I don't trust the money I'm earning," he told me. "I mean, it could be here today, gone tomorrow. I'm confident in my talent, but I've already seen other people flash through the sky, and I mean flash."

Interesting fact about Derek was that he was homosexual. He told me that early and for the right, if unusual, reason. "Don't start making any plan for me that involves a wife, kids, any of that stuff. I'm gay. I'll never have those expenses. And I'll never support a boyfriend. I live with one now, we each pay our own way and that's how it'll always be with me."

His immediate problem was cash, and I saw two places he might get some: the bank and his father.

His father was not wealthy, but he had a fair amount of money saved. The man was living in Phoenix, retired at the age of fifty-four because of emphysema. In fact, Derek told me, his father was totally disabled and collecting SSI, or Supplemental Security Income, Social Security benefits before the normal retirement age. Beyond Social Security, he lived on his savings.

I suggested a plan to Derek that I've used with a number of clients who needed capital and whose parents had reasonable savings: He should borrow $15,000 from his father and pay him 2% more interest than the bank would pay. That way Derek could take the interest payments as a deduction from his taxes, and his father would earn more on his money.

I also told him that he should try to get a loan of $25,-000 from his bank so we'd have a total of $40,000 to work with.

His father was delighted to go along with the loan. "He thinks I'm finally growing up," Derek told me, "doing some planning with my money."

The bank was hardly so friendly. To them Derek was a young, self-employed, single man in a flashy, unstable business. Even though he showed them tax returns for three years and they could see how his income was shooting up year after year, the banker said, "Yes, but how do we know what you'll be earning next year or the year after that?"

Banks tend to place most self-employed people on a level with armed robbers. Not only do bankers have business problems with the uncertainties of a free-lancer's earnings (as opposed to those of a salaried person who has held the same job for years), they also have emotional problems comprehending such an unstructured way of living.

Still, bankers do overcome their emotions if they think they can make some money by doing so, and this man could see from Derek's numbers, the letter from his agent sketching projected contracts and earnings, and a portfolio of Derek's impressive work — some of which the banker had seen in magazines — that there was potential business here. He asked Derek if he could put up any collateral against a loan. But Derek had no stocks or property, of course. We needed the loan to get him some of that.

As a last resort, he then suggested a cosigner. Did Derek know anyone with enough credit and/or the kind of steady job and substantial salary the bank would be comfortable with who would be willing to cosign the loan, taking co-responsibility for its payment?

For Derek that was easy. He turned to his boyfriend and roommate, who owned a very successful art-restoring business and had considerable inherited wealth as well.

When his boyfriend cosigned the loan application, I had Derek take out a decreasing term insurance policy on himself with the boyfriend as beneficiary. It was worth $25,000 (the amount of the loan) to start with and would decrease in value each year as the amount of the loan to be repaid decreased. But if Derek died before the whole loan was paid off, his boyfriend wouldn't be stuck with a big bank bill. It's a device I normally use with loans, usually when there is a family member, a spouse, who needs the protection.

So we now had our $40,000 for investments. In addition, as part of his plan, I got him to buy some disability insurance. About the only spot of personal vulnerability he had was the chance that he might become disabled and unable to work. He had no dependents to protect, nor would he have any, but he did have to protect himself.

Through a photographers' association, he had a small policy that would pay him $250 a week. He needed more, so I got him a policy that would add about $1000 a month to that and cost him only $400 a year in premiums.

Incidentally, there were a few provisions I made certain he had in this policy that you should try to get in your own disability policy. It was noncancellable. It was guaranteed renewable. And it covered Derek for *his occupation* until he was sixty-five.

The importance of the first two points is self-evident. Being covered in your occupation is trickier. Some disability policies will pay you for five years if you are unable to work at your occupation. After that, they might be off the hook if you can work at some other occupation. I once heard of a surgeon who lost a hand in an auto accident. He couldn't operate, but he could teach, and that's what he did, for about one-fifth of his normal earnings. His disability insurer paid him for five years, then wished him well. Their policy said, in effect, if he could earn money by some other means than his primary occupation, then he was not fully disabled and they did not have to pay him after five years.

Understandably at his age, Derek resisted the idea of retirement programs. But I showed him how, as a single resident of New York, he was being taxed as heavily as anyone in America. By setting up both an IRA and a Keogh, we could defer the taxes on tens of thousands of dollars every year and build up a substantial fund for him in his later years. And I assured him that no matter how young and invincible he felt now, he would not always be that way.

I would start feeding the IRA and Keogh from his current earnings and use his loans largely for two other pieces in the plan.

First, a tax shelter. We needed a sizable chunk of cash for that, probably $15,000 to $20,000 in the first year for the kind of real estate shelter I'd put him in.

With the balance of his borrowed $40,000, I'd open a stock market account, and we'd try to make monthly contributions to it.

There was no question that Derek would have some great opportunities to build his assets and make himself solidly wealthy as he earned big and we managed his money so he could keep the bulk of it. But once again, to get the whole thing started, he needed to borrow money.

Dealing with a less happy problem

Both Derek and Diane shared the nice problem of sudden wealth. But that is hardly the only reason why it might be smart to go into debt to launch a financial plan. Another client had a different kind of problem, one that in fact might be more widespread.

Henry Merlot was a kind of computer genius and he also knew quite a lot about music. He wanted to be a great composer, naturally, but quickly settled for something else in the music world. Henry mixed music. He could take one track of sound from a bass player and blend that with a track from a vocalist and wrap that with one from a pianist, and what came out often was a best-selling popular record.

He lived in L.A., and without pushing himself he could easily earn $125,000 in a year. Usually he didn't push himself. Besides composing his own music and trying to create new computer games, Henry would rather play chess than sit in a sound studio. When he stirred a bit, his earnings went to $200,000. Figure an average of $150,000.

Henry's problems started with Wife 1 ($20,000 a year in alimony, none of which was deductible) and the fact that Henry's idea of normal living was completely Hollywood. I don't think, single or married, he ever ate a meal in his own home. He could easily spend $150 a night for dinner and a visit to some club where one of his show-biz friends was performing. It goes without saying he drove a Mercedes.

It was Wife-to-Be 2, an unemployed actress, who sent Henry to me. Though apparently she liked the good life too, she could see that without some control there wasn't going to be much of anything for them to share. (Or, to be terribly cynical, maybe she wanted to protect her own future alimony.)

Very quickly, I could see that Henry was extremely bright and knowledgeable in unsuspected areas. Computer stocks, for example. "I don't have any money to get into them," he told me, "but I dig their machines, you know, so I got their annual reports and started to track them in the market."

I thought I saw a nice opening. "That's great, Henry," I said cheerfully. "We ought to be able to figure a way to put all that knowledge to work for you."

"What do you mean 'to work'? Invest?"

I nodded.

He removed his aviator glasses with the beige lenses and stared at me, actually looked me over for quite a while, saying nothing. "Stanley, I can beat them all."

"You can beat them all?"

"There isn't a computer game I can't beat, man, and that includes every chess program out there."

"I see," I said, but I didn't. I was missing something here.

"You invest in losers, Stanley? Not me."

I had heard worse reasons for not investing in certain stocks. "Whatever you say, Henry. Anyway, there are a lot of things we should do before we get to highly speculative stocks."

"I'm here because of my old lady, Stanley. Tell me what to do."

"We've got a couple of problems, Henry," I said. "First, getting started, and then, keeping things going."

"That's life," he said.

I knew with Henry I'd have to use the envelope technique. I give him envelopes, twelve of them, each with a date across the back (April 1, May 1, June 1, and so on), and each month he sends me an agreed-upon amount. I don't usually do that with clients, but I could see from the way Henry handled his money, it was one of our only hopes. "Henry? Could you send me something every month?" I asked him.

"Send you something? Like money, Stanley?" he said. He thought for a moment. "I don't know, to be honest with you.

I mean, I've never done anything like that."

I didn't push my luck. I explained that what I wanted most of all was to make him worth something. "All this income you earn doesn't mean anything if it all evaporates every year."

"That's what my old lady says too," he replied. "I call it treading water."

"Let me tell you what I think we can do about it," I said, and I laid out a four-part plan, though I must confess I felt a little self-conscious being so specific and organized with Henry. An IRA and a Keogh to start. Then an account in common stocks, which I'd manage aggressively. And a real estate tax shelter.

Henry listened, mostly chewing on the frame of his glasses, asking a good question here and there. He knew what I was talking about.

He nodded slowly several times when I had finished. "Sounds good, Stanley. You're going to do all that on what I can send you every month?"

"I have a feeling, given what you'd probably send me, that neither of us would live long enough if we did it that way."

"I have a feeling you're right."

I told him the best thing would be a bank loan, and given his earnings in recent years, I thought he could get $30,000. In addition, I suggested he send me $2500 a month.

"I'll even give you the envelopes, stamped yet. All you have to do is write the check on the first of each month and mail it off."

"Two and a half big ones a month, Stanley, is $30,000 a year," he said slowly.

"Nothing much for someone who earns what you do."

"I've never ended up a year with $30,000 in my life. Where's it going to come from?"

"Henry, I don't tell people how to live their lives. But if I may make a suggestion, Henry, you do spend an awful lot of money on entertainment."

"You mean food?"

"Well, restaurants."

"You want me to stop eating?"

"As I said, I don't like to tell people how to live their lives. But do you have to eat out every night?"

"Takeout is cheaper, you mean?"

"Henry, some people actually cook for themselves. Some of my wealthiest clients, Henry, believe it or not, cook their own dinners."

He looked at me pensively. "I don't know how."

"Perhaps your lady friend?"

"I like that, Stanley," he said, smiling. "I'll ask her. I mean, it's true I'm the one who picks the restaurants. She doesn't object, mind you, but she never pushes it. What the hell. This whole thing is her big idea."

"Try it," I suggested.

"You mean to tell me, if I cut down on eating out, we can score $30,000 a year?"

"It'll help," I said. I knew that if I could get him to send me the monthly check, wherever it came from, he'd somehow adjust. And not starve.

Henry's case was a bit extreme perhaps. But many people do come to me, big earners, with very big regular expenses, like alimony and rich living. The only way we can get them off the ground is a sizable bank loan.

CHAPTER 10

*B*asic pieces and moves in the *great investment game . . . Buying stocks*

I CAN ALMOST tell when it's Dr. Miano calling. The ring has that extra jingle to it, a bit like an alarm. Dr. Miano is my worst tipaholic.

Some of my clients, like so many people who invest in the market, are terribly susceptible to tips and rumors. Fortunately, most of them check with me before they act on their great scoops. Dr. Miano is special.

Not long ago he discovered a great technical breakthrough, a surgical tool that he assured me was going to alter the course of medical history. The company that owned this invention was the hottest thing since Syntex. Not only that, but Miano's sources at the hospital had told him that the stock was about to split two for one, giving two shares for every one you held.

This was a little tougher than most of his tips, dealing as it did with his own profession, but I took a deep breath and tried.

"John, I have news for you."

"Don't try to talk me out of this one, Stanley. You've done that before. But not this time. This time I've really got the inside story."

"Okay, but I've got to tell you that this stock split has already been announced."

"What do you mean 'announced'?"

"I mean the news was on the tape two weeks ago."

My piece of intelligence did not have the desired slowing effect. "Two weeks," he gasped. "God, there's no time to waste. Stanley, buy me a thousand shares right away. This is a new Xerox."

In this case Dr. Miano was fortunate. He sold the stock five months later with only a small loss. There had been a sharp rise in the stock before Dr. Miano had ever heard of the invention. A lot of Wall Streeters had heard the story, and they gave the stock a bit of a play. Miano bought right at the high.

Information, real information in the stock market, is an extremely valuable commodity. People invest great amounts of time and energy to come up with it. Very often the inside tip that you have is already shared by thousands. Clients call me to verify tips nearly every day. My response is invariably the same: If I have already heard their inside story or can check it out in two minutes with a phone call, they probably don't want to buy the stock. What they know, under those circumstances, is very public knowledge. High technology is a particularly attractive area for rumors and tips. Like Dr. Miano, everybody is searching for the new Xerox, the next IBM. All it takes is a teeny, tiny disk, a simple process.

Nimslo was a good recent example. This company had a new development in 3-D photography, a camera that was not terribly larger than or different from an ordinary camera. But it could take 3-D pictures.

Obviously a terrific product, so terrific that the price of the stock was pushed up far beyond what it could earn from the new technology. Still, people rushed to buy. I had a flood of calls from clients with their inside news, including one from the owner of a small chain of camera stores. Normally a fairly cautious investor, he was now breathless. Like Dr. Miano and his discovery in the hospital, this man had at last heard of something in his own industry that had the trappings of a breakthrough and a killing.

Meanwhile, in the real world there were problems. The new camera was expensive and so was its film. Also, the 3-D picture was not so 3-D and it kind of faded toward the edges. The big market test came in the Christmas season of 1982, and the camera bombed. The owner of the camera chain and a few of my other clients had paper losses of about 50% within a couple of months.

Takeover stories are a big part of the rumor game. They are especially tempting because they often have elements of truth to them. Like American Express is meeting with RCA. And it turns out, let's say, they are. I can confirm that for my clients, but the rest of the story is that the meetings have nothing to do with a takeover.

Even so, the temptation of being able to buy a stock at 22 today that is going to be bought out next Thursday for $38 a share — all so certain and so quick — that temptation is irresistible to so many people who are always looking for the easy road to big money.

You can make big money in the stock market. In fact, as a planner I look at stocks as the premier investment to make capital grow. Rarely, however, do you make big money through tips and prayers and rolling the dice. There are techniques and systems, ways to make rational and intelligent market decisions.

You can even apply sense to those rumors. The next time you hear an exciting, guaranteed takeover story, reach for the nearest chart of that stock. (We'll discuss charts later in this chapter.) Well, well, that's interesting. The chart shows that several weeks ago the stock suddenly rose in price. It went from $30 to $42, and $42 is where you can buy it today. The stock has, as we say on Wall Street, 12 points of takeover built into its price.

All of which tells you two solid things: An awful lot of

other people knew about this supposed takeover before you. And if you buy that stock at 42 and there is no takeover, you're going to see that stock drop 12 points with the speed of sound.

Let's consider an approach to buying stocks that's based on judgment derived from information. It's not infallible, but you'll do much better with it than tossing your money after whispers and fads.

The search for growth stocks

We go from the general to the particular. Our perspective is derived from studying first the overall market, then industry groups within the market and then individual stocks within those groups. Ideally what we want is the best stock in the most-favored industry group in a rising market.

A great new bull market, the likes of which we have not seen in decades, began in August of 1982. Stocks rose sharply and uninterruptedly for many months. This rise was greeted with the usual diversity of opinion. Some people doubted the whole thing and "fought the tape" all the way up. Others became euphoric after many months of sharp rises and thought they could buy just about anything and make money.

It was unquestionably a time to buy, and a time to buy growth stocks. Those are the ones that bring us the most profit. So we move from our view of the market at large to a consideration of industries and groups within the market where we will find the most promising growth stocks.

Some clients of mine who maintain rather casual relationships with the market have quaint ideas of what growth industries and growth stocks are. They prefer the household names, like RCA and Xerox. RCA was a great growth company in the 1920s, but it has not really succeeded in staying abreast of major areas of growth in recent years. Xerox certainly was once a great growth company, but today photo-copying machines are as common as mimeograph machines were in the forties, and in some areas the competition has surpassed Xerox's technology. Years ago I sold Polaroid for several clients at $130 a share. In May 1982 it was $30 a share without a single split, but some people still think that Polaroid is a great growth company.

There are mature industries whose fortunes rise and fall with the economic cycle, and at certain points in the cycle you can make money on their stocks. But these are not really what we are looking for. The stocks of manufacturing companies, "smokestack America" companies like US Steel and Goodyear Tire, don't excite me. In our post-industrial society, manufacturing steel or tires no longer represents growth. Every auto that is produced in this country has steel parts and rubber tires, but these industries have long passed their period of great growth.

Growth in America today lies in high technology, communications and services. Computers, computer software, electronics, robotics, satellite communications, medical technology — these and many others like them are the stuff of the future.

When we consider individual companies in such fields as these, we see patterns of development. First a stage of relative quiet. The company is just developing its particular product or service, just getting itself organized and finding its market.

Then there is a kind of takeoff period, a time of accelerating growth, when the business expands and the earnings increase rapidly.

Finally, there is a stage of maturity. The company's product or service is no longer new or unique. Its market is no longer expanding and its competition is gaining on it. The company may very well continue to earn profits, but its stock price will probably cease to climb. This growth stock has now become a cyclical stock. It will go up when the economy is expanding and the market is rising, and it will decline in recessions and bad markets, but it no longer has a persistent upward trend.

You might also find one part of an industry or a company that has matured while at the same time spawning new products with growth potential. The main portion of IBM's business was the development and sale of large mainframe computers. That part of its business has already matured. Yet the computer business grows wonderfully. Now we have minicomputers, distributed data processing word processors, portable computers, computer-aided design and manufacturing. IBM has moved into most of these areas and still grows. But younger companies, exclusively dedicated to the expanding areas of the business, can grow faster.

To me the purest growth industry would be a service business that is involved with advanced technology. And that brings us to hospital management companies. They run hospitals, so they offer services to patients and are involved with the newest medical technology, everything from CAT scanners to quadruple-bypass operations to new drugs.

I have been buying hospital management stocks since January 1975. I've owned large positions in the stocks of a number of companies, including National Medical Enterprises, Brookwood Health Services, American Medicorp, American Medical International and several others. They have all been spectacular successes. Over the years several have quadrupled in price and many have been taken over at large profits.

When to buy

The growth in the hospital management field is so extensive that many of these stocks remain, after all of these years, excellent buys. But there are new, younger companies in the field that have more promise than the established companies. And never forget that this process will not go on forever.

The day will come when the hospital business will be as stodgy and uninspiring as steel-making or coal-mining.

To pick a winner, you need a sense of timing. You have to grasp where your stock stands in the growth cycle of its industry and in the overall market cycle. Growth means the future: You buy a stock because of what you expect it will do. That a stock has done well today, yesterday, for the last year, only matters insofar as that performance gives you a clue to what is going to happen tomorrow. But you should not buy a stock on the basis of what it has already done.

As obvious as this seems, think about the number of times you bought a stock because of a strong recent showing, only to find that the stock ceased to move at all after you bought it.

The market anticipates what the earnings and progress of a company will be. When you buy a stock today for $20 a share, you should know enough about that company to believe that its future earnings and general performance will make clear that it is really worth $30 a share. If you have chosen intelligently, the stock will indeed move up to $30, and by that time perhaps it will be possible to anticipate further progress for the company and a rise to $40.

Just when you buy that stock also relates to those stages of development I spoke of.

Everyone wants to find the great growth situation before anyone else. Everyone wants to get in on the famous ground floor. Well, if you had gotten in on the ground floor of Xerox, you would have bought something called Haloid Corporation, a company stalled in an unpromising branch of the photography business. Searching for a new product, this company connected with Dr. Anton Carlson, who needed money to finance a process that would become known as xerography. For years money and research were funneled into Dr. Carlson's efforts, with meager results. Then, finally, the Xerox process of photocopying became a commercial reality. Haloid had changed its name to Xerox, and the stock took off in one of the market's great historic advances.

But what happened if you were in on the real ground floor? You bought Haloid in 1956 when xerography was mostly a dream in Dr. Carlson's mind. Three years later, your miracle stock was trading at a third of what you had paid for it and you were yelling at your broker for sticking you with a dog. Sell, you told him, I'll take it for a tax loss.

Alas, you bought in the development stage. Not long after you sold, the curve started to turn up as the company entered its takeoff period.

Perhaps the effect of your blowing it with Xerox was to leave you forever sniffing for revenge. You finally found your chance a few years ago. Three guys in a garage in California were making a sophisticated electronic device. You not only had your personal Xerox experience under your belt, you now had the public tale of Apple. Another guy, another garage.

You buy. Only this time, you do not rush in alone. You wait, you watch, you see the stock starting to rise.

You buy, confident that this time you are in on the development stage. You are right, except there is no development stage. Turns out the three guys in the garage make terrific electronic devices, but not one of them knows anything about running a business.

You are poorer but, let us hope, wiser. You should know by now that you do not make money by buying stock in the great industry of the future if the future lies seven or eight years ahead. For one thing, you might guess wrong. Or guess right about the industry and find that the company you have chosen goes bankrupt instead of through the heavens.

Good values

When and what you buy is further linked to what you have to pay for your stock. Is it a good value?

One of the ways you decide is the price/earnings ratio (P/E ratio) of the stock. It is printed along with your stock in the day's stock market listings and derived by dividing the earnings per share that your company has realized in the past twelve months into the current price of the stock.

If the company you are considering earned $4 a share during the last four quarters, and the stock now sells for $48, it has a P/E ratio of 12. It is, in other words, selling for twelve times earnings.

Does that make it a good value? Depends. Compare that ratio with the P/E ratio of similar companies in other lively businesses. More important, consider what the future earnings of your company are estimated to be. What's the P/E ratio based on next year's earnings? As I continually tell my clients, the stock market is all anticipation.

Your stock might be selling for thirty times earnings and still not be overpriced. Let's say it is $15 a share and has earned only 50¢ a share in the past twelve months. At thirty times earnings, it seems pretty scary. But if your information is that this company is going to earn $1.50 a share, then it is only selling at ten times future earnings and maybe it is a buy.

Then too, your stock might be a high-multiple stock in a high-multiple group, such as computers, and perhaps in a strongly advancing market. The reality then is that the group and all of the promising companies in the group are selling at thirty times earnings because the general opinion is that future earnings will justify such a multiple. Still, if your price is something like fifty times earnings, you know that you are taking a big risk. It would take extraordinary growth in earnings to justify such a lofty P/E.

It's possible to talk not only about the individual P/Es of stocks but also of the market as a whole. In past decades, bull markets topped out when the Dow-Jones Industrials were at something like twenty to twenty-four times earnings. New bull markets began when the Dow's P/E was as low as seven or eight times earnings. But this is no guaranteed guide to when bull markets begin and end. In particular, up through the decade of the seventies, it appeared that P/E ratios at market tops were getting lower and lower. My guess is that the eighties will bring higher numbers.

Making decisions about stocks and the market is no easy task. You should expect a lot of help from your broker. He should be experienced and sophisticated enough to make sound judgments and be able to explain to you how they were derived. Unless you are in a position to devote a great deal of time and effort to the task, you have two choices: You can let your broker run the show entirely or you can participate in the process with him. If you want to be involved and the broker doesn't give you the kinds of comparisons and evaluations I've mentioned, get a new broker.

Most people do depend on the judgment and research of their broker and his firm. But that doesn't mean you have to throw yourself on his mercy. You do not have to be ignorant and watch him plunk your money down wherever he wants. Shortly I will recommend a number of magazines, newspapers, other sources of information, that you can use to become an informed customer. You can, and really must be able to, ask the right questions and evaluate your broker's or planner's answers and performance.

Still, you remain an amateur, a part-time amateur at that. And, as we'll see, to make a truly informed decision on a stock takes an awful lot of time, as well as access to people and data that you simply don't have. So let me describe my own process of analysis as one approach that has brought reasonable success. Not that I would suggest for a moment that mine is the only method, but as I said, it is one that has worked well. And if you pick out parts of it that engage you and ask your broker about his own approach, he might respond by spreading out a different system, and one that seems satisfactory to you, especially if his results have been satisfactory. Still, you will have gained new respect from that broker for even asking the questions you did. And you will lift yourself a step closer to the whole process.

Fundamentalists versus technicians

It's rather simplistic, but experts on stocks and the market are generally divided into two camps: the fundamentalists and the technicians.

The fundamentalists analyze everything about a company — the product it makes, its potential market, the company's management — and how all of this relates to the broader questions of the nation's economy and the world beyond.

Technical analysts maintain that all there is to know about a stock is already manifested in the price and volume patterns the stock has traced out in its past trading. The chart tells all, if you know how to read the chart. No need to bother with management or anything as vague and distant as "the economy."

Technicians study not only charts of individual stocks but charts of many different market groups. And they also review vast quantities of statistics and monitor a great many seemingly esoteric market indicators, like odd-lot short sales, advisory-sentiment index, mutual fund cash balances, insider buying and selling, and the overbought-oversold index.

When I select stocks, I combine both approaches. I never buy a stock on any basis but sound fundamentals. I always keep in mind that what really works is to have the right stock in the right industry in the right kind of market, and that means a solid analysis of fundamentals. The quality of a company's management is of great importance to me. However, I will never buy a stock, no matter how sound the fundamentals, without first reviewing its chart. If its chart pattern is adverse, I won't buy. Such a chart tells me that somebody knows something I don't know or I overlooked in my research, and I am always grateful for the warning.

Also, the chart gives me a good historical perspective on the stock. Did it fall along with everything else during a broad drop in the stock market? Sometimes a chart that indicates a stock went down less than most stocks during a decline is giving you a hint: It will go up more than most during the forthcoming advance. I also want to see what the recent chart pattern has been in the stock, and I want to know where the "support levels" and the "resistance levels" are and what a "consolidation pattern" in this stock looks like. (More on these in the next chapter.)

But as I've said, I am first of all a fundamentalist. I read everything I can find on the company I'm considering. My assistant calls the company's investor contact and gets their annual report, quarterly report, 10K (a special tax report that is sent to the federal government) and a great deal of other material. If the company has offered securities in the recent past, I'll read the prospectus of that offering. I'll also read all of the reports that have been written on the company by security analysts or advisory services.

Direct contact with the officers of the corporation is valuable. Frequently I'll call the president or treasurer of the company I'm considering and get a closer reading of the operation and of the people running it. A useful step, and one that is not available to the nonprofessional. They won't take your call.

Often I can also question executives at analysts' sessions or at "due diligence" meetings for stock offerings. Again, this sort of thing isn't generally available to members of the public, but I find it invaluable. Nothing gives me a stronger opinion of a company than seeing that its management is of high quality, and these gatherings offer me a good chance to judge.

I recall, for example, a number of years ago I attended a meeting given by Mego, a toy company listed on the American Stock Exchange. It was a time when toy stocks were in vogue, and from a distance Mego looked good. As a result of the meeting I kept away from the stock. I was extremely unimpressed by the man who was president. His presentation seemed disorganized, and when it came to questions from the floor, he seemed quite uninformed.

Electronic games, for instance, were just becoming important then, and when he was asked what Mego was going to do with this market, he said, in a most roundabout way, that they were thinking of looking into it. Everybody in the room knew that electronic games were the fastest-growing area of the toy world and that some of Mego's competitors were already well along in that end of the business.

So I never bought the stock, and when I heard some years later that Mego had gone bankrupt, I was hardly surprised. To be sure, toys are a tough business, subject to waves of fads. All the more need for sharp management and sharp judgment on the part of the investor.

Another toy company I looked at sometime after Mego was Coleco. Quite a different story. I was extremely impressed with their top people.

Coleco went on to make a ton of money selling games and game cassettes. Their stock soared. In 1982, it was one of the single biggest winners in the stock market.

But as I said, this is a tough business, subject to waves of fads. After a while it became clear that game cassettes would be something like records: Out of one hundred, one or two would sell phenomenally and ninety-eight would lose money.

Coleco and countless other toy companies had problems. And here's where Coleco's good management made a difference: They attempted a transition to home computers, an effort that has been difficult and rocky for them, but which has given them a new chance. (They have also kept active in the children's market. As this book goes to press, they are riding what might be their biggest wave ever — the Cabbage Patch dolls.)

As for me and my own sharp management? I bought the

stock years ago, made large profits on it. But I sold too soon. I am, I told you, a hard-working fundamental analyst and a technical analyst. I am also a human being. I don't understand fads. As an investor, they frighten me. As the cassette fad was cresting, I bailed out.

Another blunder that I made was with a computer company, Mohawk Data Sciences. I spotted Mohawk in the early stages of the 1982–83 upward move in the market. It seemed to me to be grossly undervalued. Mohawk, doing 45% of its business in Europe, was hurt by exchange-rate problems at the time, the dollar being so strong. I assumed that Washington would do something about the extreme strength of the dollar, that economic recovery in Europe would help and that this would aid companies doing lots of business in Europe. Well, it didn't happen, and my Mohawk stock languished at a time when other computer stocks were soaring.

So picking winners in the market involves being right about everything from the quality of management to the nature of world economic trends.

But the best management in the world can't prevail against unfavorable economics or unfavorable demographics. I don't care who the head of US Steel is; the fact is that his corporation controls billions of dollars of obsolete plant and equipment and faces tough foreign competition. Continuous casting and other sophisticated manufacturing techniques might help a bit, but the steel industry in the United States just isn't a growth business anymore, hasn't been for many, many years and can't ever become one again.

Are you helpless?

I have tried to sketch my approach to the stock market and selecting stocks. I've been brief and overly simple, but I hope that I have given you some sense of what a time-consuming and complex business it can be.

My clients tend to run to extremes. There are those who leave everything to me and those who participate heavily in picking stocks.

But I think they are all honest about their own feelings toward risk. There is always risk involved when you buy stocks, and you are always acting on the basis of insufficient information. (If you ever find it otherwise, if you find yourself confronting the sure thing, duck.)

If my clients want me to make all the decisions, they at least define the level of risk they want. Will they buy over-the-counter stocks? Very aggressive stocks? More conservative stocks? Do they want a margin account or a cash account?

Those who get involved in the process of picking stocks make a real effort to inform themselves. I recommend to them and to you a number of sources of information.

Read *The Wall Street Journal* every day. I like its column of daily market reporting, the summary of business news, its comprehensive articles on all business.

Read *Barron's Weekly*. It has a good discussion on the trading action of the market, other newsworthy feature stories and a formidable collection of market statistics.

Forbes is helpful with its reviews of individual companies, and the columns in the back of the magazine, where experts select stocks, can broaden your own perspective.

I also recommend *Business Week, Fortune* and *U.S. News & World Report,* among other magazines. The *Wall Street Transcript* is a weekly publication in newspaper format that reprints market letters and the individual stock reports of many brokerage firms. It provides a wealth of information, although when you read a report there, you are getting it weeks after the client of the brokerage firm.

As a monthly, *Money* magazine cannot be very current on the market, but a number of my clients find it useful in broader matters of financial planning.

The *Value Line Survey* ranks industry groups in order of

their market promise, and within those groups ranks many hundreds of stocks by potential market performance. I like that approach, and *Value Line* has done a good job in picking winners in bull markets. However, their analysts don't study companies as intensively as brokerage analysts do.

When it comes to newsletters, I have a problem, or maybe it's inherent to the beast. Ever since I became a broker in 1966, there have been a handful of hot market letters at any given time, and they tend to burn out and vanish altogether. A few of the most widely read and quoted letters of 1966 no longer exist. I look at dozens of market letters and often learn something from them. I can't recommend any outright, but lately *Professional Tape Reader* and *The Zweig Forecast* have done well.

Your broker should provide you with the reports written by his firm's analysts. Beyond the recommendation and the analysis of a particular stock, these reports provide you with essential data: last year's earnings, this year's earnings, projections for next year, figures on P/E ratios among other important data, and a chart of the stock.

Learn to read charts. There are several books on technical analysis that are worth reading. *Technical Analysis of Stock Trends,* by Robert D. Edwards and John McGee, is the best book. *Granville's New Strategy of Daily Stock Market Timing for Maximum Profit,* by Joseph Granville, and *Stock Market Logic: A Sophisticated Approach to Profits on Wall Street,* by Norman G. Fosback, are two other substantial books.

For a basic introduction to the market, read *How to Buy Stocks,* by Louis Engle with Peter Wykoff. *Security Analysis: Principles and Techniques,* by Benjamin Graham, is the basic work on the measurement of value in the stock market.

CHAPTER 11

M^{ore} *on stocks . . . When to sell*

ONCE UPON A TIME there was a man named Bernard
Baruch. Mr. Baruch made a fortune in the market and he
also enjoyed publicity. Part of his image was friendly adviser,
a guy who sat on a park bench and answered your questions.
"How can I do it, Mr. Baruch?" the bent widow asks him.
"How can I make a fortune in the market like you?"
"My dear lady," the wise man replies, "buy low and sell
high. Let your profits run and cut your losses."
Whereupon that widow found her way to my office and
said, "See, Stanley, it's simple. Do as the great man says.
Make me a fortune."
Or so it sometimes seems, given the number of people
who quote me that clichéd wisdom. But getting from the idea
to the reality is usually left to me.
How, in fact, can you know that your stock has run its
course? That you won't be selling too soon if you get out of
a stock that has brought you a substantial profit? How do you
know that your stock, which has just dropped a couple of
points, is really on the way down? That it has not merely
dipped and is about to rise sharply once again? In other
words, how do you know when to sell?
If you are like my actress client, whom I'll call Monica
Sheridan, you have a simple formula and keep changing it.
Monica evolved her original formula during one of those

long stretches when she was between engagements, which is when she is most involved with her investments. Over the years Monica has not done badly in the market, especially considering the scores of brokers she has used and discarded — including one ex-husband — and the scores of theories she has evolved and tested.

"My problem, Stanley darling," she said one day, "is that I get so emotional about my stocks. Sometimes it breaks my heart to sell them."

And she was right. She got trapped in stocks that dropped and dropped because she had such high hopes when she bought them, and got so attached to them, that when they dropped she decided it would be better to wait. Eventually, someday, that darling stock would simply have to go back up.

That's called getting "locked in," an extremely widespread disease on Wall Street. It was to avoid that disease that Monica came up with her first formula for me.

"Darling, this can't miss," she declared with her theatrical bravado. "From now on here's what we're going to do: We're going to let all our profits ride up to 30% ... okay?"

"I'm listening."

"And we're going to limit our losses to 10%," she continued. "Isn't that heaven?"

"It is heaven, Monica," I told her. "Absolute heaven. But it won't work."

"It's got to work, Stanley darling. I just know it will work."

I tried to explain as gently as I could. First, why be arbitrary about those profits? If we've selected a stock wisely, a growth stock that's got years to build before it starts to level off, and we're buying at an early point in a developing bull market, then we might see profits reaching beyond 300%. Why throw away all those gains because the formula says stop at 30%?

What's more, I've never seen a 300% advance, or even a 100% advance, that wasn't interrupted by a number of corrections. Those corrections are quite variable. Sometimes they last for many months, sometimes for only a few weeks. And most of them are more than 10%. So if Monica held to her sell-after-a-10%-drop formula, she would *never* have a big winner in the market.

Monica listened. "You might have a point, Stanley," she replied. "You just might. I'll tell you what. Why don't we change our sell formula? Give ourselves a bit more time when those dreary corrections come along? Why don't we say we'll sell if our losses reach 15%, rather than 10%?"

"But suppose we hit a bear market and your stocks drop and we sell after we've lost 15%?" I said. "So we buy something else, and the something else also drops 15%. And maybe the same thing happens a third time and a fourth time."

This left her perplexed and somewhat confused. "Monica, please, listen to me," I told her. "Lots of people use formulas like yours, and on paper they're all winners, sure winners. But in fact, it never works out that way."

She said she wanted to think it over. A few days later, she had a new variation on her formula. My response was the same: The arbitrary, mechanical approach to market timing doesn't work.

My approach to selling is an extension of my approach to buying. I look at my stock in relation to the whole market, to the group of stocks it is in, and use both fundamental and technical analysis for guidance.

Where is the overall market going? Is it going up while my stock, bought just weeks ago, is dropping? How is this group doing? Did we simply make a mistake a few weeks ago?

What's been happening to the company since we bought the stock? Are there rumors that the next quarter is going to be bad? Did the company fail to get a contract that we thought was a sure thing? How serious is its announcement that there's going to be a delay of four months on that new plant?

In other words, if my stock is going down, I first do a re-examination of the assumptions that I made when I bought it.

Bring in the charts

I've also got to examine the chart of this troubled stock, because in fact it might reveal to me that there is nothing to worry about.

Looking over the stock's history, I might see that it frequently fluctuates six to eight points. If that is the case, I had better not sell it simply because it is down three points.

Or I might find that although the stock had dropped, it is still one point above a "support level." That is what forms when a stock trades in some volume and for some time in a narrow range of prices. If it moves upward for a while and then drops back later on, it may find support where it had traded for so long before. People will respond to it at that price level. "I could have bought it at 20," they'll say, "then the thing went up to 27. Now I've got my chance again. It's dropped down to 21."

Or if the stock went down instead of up after trading heavily for some time (let's say up around 20 and dropped to 15), then rose again, we would see a "resistance level" when it re-approached 20. This time investors who had bought around 20 would sigh happily as the stock rebounded. "I'm even," they'd say, and sell.

So if I look at the chart and see my stock is down but still above a support level, I can say, "Let's wait. Let's see if the support level holds." To be sure, you can't always find a support level on the chart of a stock, but when you do, it is a lot more reliable as a guide for selling than some arbitrary percentage of decline.

Or maybe what I see is a "consolidation pattern." Chart patterns basically divide into two sorts: consolidation patterns and reversal patterns. Reversal means just what it says: a change of direction from up to down or vice versa. But a consolidation pattern shows that the stock is merely pausing. It will resume its move in the same direction as before once the consolidation ends. When I see that, I know that I don't have to worry as long as that pattern is not broken, but I do have to decide how patient I want to be.

However, if the chart of the stock indicates real trouble, I will probably sell. I will review the fundamentals to see if they provide some rationale for the ominous chart pattern, but whether they do or not I generally won't argue with the chart. I'll sell for defensive reasons.

Again, all of my decisions are made against my overall perception of the market, and as much as I possibly can, I try to be in gear with the market cycle. In the best of all possible worlds, you want to sell out just before the bull market ends.

Unfortunately, *The Wall Street Journal* doesn't publish a calendar: "TEN DAYS TO END OF BULL MARKET . . . ONLY TEN SELLING DAYS LEFT." So once again, reading the charts is crucial, if not infallible.

In the best of all possible worlds, we are buying growth stocks early in the bull market and holding them through the entire stretch. If a client has a tax situation where he can afford to take some short-term gains, we might sell something for a quick profit if it has moved up sharply, or we might lighten up to sidestep a correction. But we won't panic and sell everything so long as we think that the bull market is still alive. My basic strategy is to ride out any minor declines and let our profits run on in the ensuing advance.

The most famous advocate of defensive selling was the same Mr. Bernard Baruch. When a reporter asked him how he made money in the market, Baruch answered, "By selling too soon." He got out of the market in 1928.

How do you know when a bull market is ending? That is

the toughest question of all. I suppose Mr. Baruch judged by using fundamental standards of evaluation. He sold when he thought stocks were fully valued or approaching overvaluation.

It is good to remember that the stock market is a creature of extremes. At the lows, stocks sell for less than they are worth, and fear and despair are everywhere. At the highs, everyone is euphoric and everyone is buying. This is when you get tips from hairdressers, cab drivers and elevator operators. When that happens, it is time to head for the exits.

Technical analysis of the market is helpful in timing your sale. A number of major bull markets of the past ended with clear-cut reversal patterns in the Dow-Jones Industrial Average. One spectacular occurrence was back in 1962. In March, the Dow had completed a "head and shoulders top," which often signals the end of a major move. Some days after that reversal pattern was completed, President Kennedy attacked Roger Blough, then head of US Steel, for not holding the line on prices. The market actually rose for a few days after the speech and then dropped straight down. It was widely assumed that Kennedy's attack on US Steel specifically, and on big business in general, indicated that his administration would be bad for business. So, a bear market.

I didn't accept that idea at all. The chart of the Dow signaled the bear market and I sold out my entire portfolio. The bear market was, in my view, a reflection of fundamentals that went deeper than the effects of one speech by the President.

When to sell a winner

At the end of the bull market.

It may sound like a parody of our friend Baruch, but actually that's what we're trying to do.

If we pick our stocks right, and our timing in terms of the

whole market is at all accurate, we should have a chance at a long run. Monica Sheridan's 30% gain is not so terrible, but 300% is so much nicer.

I bought Berg Enterprises at 5¾ in 1982. The stock split three for two, and in June of 1983 it was 33¼ after the split. A colleague had sold it at 11. "I've practically doubled my money," he told me contentedly.

I didn't sell at 11 because Berg's chart showed an unbroken uptrend, because we were in the early stages of a new bull market and because Berg, a real estate and mortgage banking company, was a prominent beneficiary of the economic recovery. The chart, the market and the company all told me to hold.

Holding stocks during drops can make for some nervous times. Recently PTR (Professional Tape Reader), one of the most successful advisory services, issued a strong warning: Sell Telex. The stock was at 22 and PTR said that the chart pattern indicated the game was over.

I had bought that stock at 7 in 1982, so I had already tripled my clients' money. But I didn't sell, because I read the stock's chart differently. I saw it as a consolidation pattern and not a reversal. In truth, I was not very comfortable with my decision because I respect PTR. But in the end I felt I had to be faithful to my own interpretation. Happily, I was right, and the stock reached a new high of 31½ some months after PTR said sell.

There are times when astronomic rises should be viewed with alarm. I bought National Video in 1965 at 44¾ and two months later it was 150. At the end, the stock was moving straight up, 6 or 8 points a day. This is what Wall Street calls a "blowoff," and I wanted to sell because it was clear that a collapse was imminent. On the day the stock hit 150, I sold. By the time my sell order was executed, the stock was 137. But I was still extremely fortunate. A week later it was selling at 98, and a year later the company was bankrupt.

Even if you don't use charts, you can use common sense with a stock like that. Let's say that you buy a stock at 10 and two weeks later it has jumped to 15. You've got a 50% gain, which is fine, but a little arithmetic will tell you something else. If this meteoric rise keeps on at 50% every two weeks, your hand calculator will show you that in sixteen weeks your stock will be selling for 256. Not very likely.

If the client knows best

"Sell, Stanley, sell," comes the familiar cry, and if I disagree I try hard to convince my client and I by no means always win.

I am not always right, but I do at least make my moves in the market with care and for what I consider good reasons. So often when clients call with that plea, they are scared or acting on the great wisdom of a tennis buddy. To be sure, if you've already made a nice profit in a stock, your brain might coolly register the value of riding out a further advance, but your nerves say, "Enough is enough. The greedy shall be punished." It's not easy.

I had a recent situation like that with Monica Sheridan and Wang Laboratories. She had bought a hundred shares in the high 20s in the summer of 1982. By spring 1983, Wang had split two for one, was selling for $38 a share and Monica and my other clients who owned it had more than doubled their money.

"Why be greedy, sweetheart?" Monica asked. "I'm ecstatic at what we've done so far. Couldn't we just sell Mr. Wang and relax?"

I pointed out that if we did sell now, she wouldn't have owned it for a year, so she'd give the IRS half her profit. And beyond that, Wang is an extraordinarily well managed company that has positioned itself in those areas of computer technology, sales and service that are the most promising in the industry. To be sure, on her side of the argument, Wang had risen to a frighteningly high P/E ratio.

"Monica, let's compromise on this one. Let's sell, but not for at least two months, until it's long-term."

"Really, love? You're sure?"

"Really, Monica. Trust me."

"Stanley, darling, I do."

Happy ending. We did hold, we did get a long-term gain and Monica sold her Wang Laboratories stock at a substantial profit.

Short-term profit

Clearly to be avoided most of the time, but there are other times.

First of all, with any IRA, Keogh or pension trust, or any other kind of retirement plan, taking a short-term profit involves no tax liability. Your taxes are deferred until you start withdrawing your money from the plan. Also, with custodial accounts your child is probably in a very low tax bracket, so you don't have to be concerned about short-term gains.

Then there are people who have a tax-loss carry-forward against which short-term profits can be applied.

Sometimes the stock itself forces your hand. It shoots up, and for any number of good reasons, you know it's not going anywhere further, or worse, it's going to drop back down. Then you don't have much choice.

Fox Stanley Photo was like that. Years ago I bought it for my clients at 8⅝. It traded at that price, and with very low volume, for weeks. I had an order in every day, trying to buy the stock for my customers without driving the price up. When I finally stopped buying, Fox Stanley immediately dropped to 8, and I had a few unhappy moments noticing that I had been supporting the stock and that there were no other buyers around. But that changed abruptly. Merrill

Lynch recommended the stock, and in short order it shot up to 14. I was happy to sell all my stock to those avid Merrill Lynch customers. I made a 60% profit for my clients in a few months and was glad to have it, even though it was a short-term gain. Nearly a year later, Fox Stanley was below 14 in price.

Checklist for Chapter 11

1. The great aim, of course, is to let your profits run and cut your losses. And it can be done.

2. Avoid mechanical theories, like selling when your gains hit 30% or when you suffer a 10% loss. Life in the market is not neat and simple.

3. Make your decision about when to sell from the same perspective you applied when you bought. Look at where your stock is in relation to the whole market, to the group of stocks it's in, and use both fundamental and technical analysis for guidance.

4. Don't fall in love with your stocks. Even though they may be way up, don't be lulled by your successes. If you have a stock that has risen a great deal, ask yourself whether you would buy it today at this high a price. If your answer is no, maybe no one else would buy it either.

5. If your stock is down, reexamine your fundamental assumptions about the company. Was your judgment off? Has something important happened to the company since you bought the stock, causing it to drop?

6. Examine the stock's chart. Is its price drop no greater than previous random fluctuations? Has it reached a "support level"? Is it in a "consolidation pattern"?

7. Always keep a sharp eye on the overall market. Theoretically you should always be in gear with the market cycle. Try to buy a stock with growth potential early in a bull market and hold it till the end of the bull market.

8. If your perception of the market cycle is accurate, you

will not sell a stock that is rising until you perceive the approaching end of the bull market or it appears that your stock is going to "top out" before the rest of the market does.

9. Normally when you sell with a profit, try to time your sale so that you have owned the stock for at least a year and a day, so that you'll be taxed at the long-term capital gains rate.

CHAPTER 12

Bonds... The pleasures and perils of long-term loans

THEY'RE COMFORTING, bonds, especially to people who don't really understand them. Exuding security, protection for widows and orphans, they even offer class. Characters in drawing room comedies, pre-1929, clipped coupons and danced all night at the Stork Club.

Times change. Bonds are no longer issued with coupons to clip and turn in at your bank for cash. Today if you buy a new bond, you will still get a fixed rate of interest, say 8% a year, but instead of those classy coupons to clip, you will simply get a check in the mail, usually twice a year.

The more meaningful change to bond buyers is that "bearer bonds" are no longer issued. Bearer bonds not only had coupons attached to them, they were anonymous. Your name was not typed on the certificate. If you had one, you could stow the bond in a bank vault and usually no one but you knew what was in that vault. Every six months you visited the bank, clipped a coupon and cashed it at the teller's desk. Your privacy was preserved, and maybe you got more than privacy out of this arrangement. Maybe you gave a key to the vault to your son or daughter and warned them that if you died the vault should be cleaned out to evade estate tax on your bearer bond. Maybe your bearer bond was a taxable corporate bond, and perhaps you were one of those people who cashed the coupons without declaring the interest on your tax return. Even U.S. Treasuries fell into the category of bearer bonds on which people evaded taxes. Of course, tax evasion is subject to severe penalties if you get caught. The truth is that a lot of people didn't get caught.

Today all bonds that are issued are registered bonds. They don't have coupons that you can clip in the quiet secrecy of that little room next to the bank vault, and when you buy one, your name is registered and written on the certificate. The new requirements for registering bonds are designed to prevent taxpayers from keeping secrets from the IRS.

To be sure, billions of dollars of previously issued bearer bonds do exist. If you buy one of those today, you still have the anonymity of palmier times, but the Feds are cracking down on those old-fashioned tax-evasion practices.

Whether you have a bearer bond or a registered one, you'll collect interest regularly, year after year after year, until the bond matures in ten years, twenty years, thirty years, whatever the life of the bond. Then the company or city or state agency or whoever issued the bond will send you a check for the full amount you lent them all those years ago when you first bought the bond.

A bond is, then, a loan you make to American Tel & Tel or the Massachusetts Bay Transportation Authority, frequently for a long period of time. For the purposes of my clients, I am interested mainly in tax-exempt bonds, with certain exceptions. Regular corporate bonds might be highly rated and offer nice yields, but they are fully taxable and as we've seen elsewhere, whenever possible I want to avoid giving half that interest income to the Feds. With retirement accounts, where taxes are deferred, or custodial accounts in low tax brackets, I do recommend good taxable bonds.

I said earlier that times change. Are bonds still the paper of the rich? Yes and no.

It still takes a certain amount of capital to build an intelligent, balanced bond portfolio. You don't just snap up a bond for a few bucks. All tax-exempts today are in multiples of $5000. Corporate and utility bonds come in multiples of $1000, though you usually want to buy a much larger amount.

In terms of planning, if you come to me with a passion for bonds and only $10,000 to support your craving, I'm going to put you into a bond trust, which is similar to a mutual fund, and we'll consider them later in this chapter.

If you approach me with the same yearning and $25,000, I would still recommend a bond trust, but if you don't like that kind of arrangement, if you want more to say about which bonds to buy and you want to build your own particular portfolio, then we have a problem.

That $25,000 will merely get you started on the way to a portfolio. So if we buy Phoenix Municipal Housing bonds with your money, I will be very uncomfortable, because we have all our eggs in one basket. I will try hard to convince you to come up with another $25,000 so we can buy a completely different bond, and another $25,000 and another so we can truly diversify that portfolio.

In exchange for lending your $25,000, $10,000 or $5000 to Louisville or Des Moines, they promise to pay you interest at the rate that was set when their bonds were issued.

The rate is determined by the quality of the bonds, their ratings and the number of years till maturity. The longer you lend the state of Louisiana your money, the higher the interest they'll pay you. The general condition of the market will affect the pricing of the bonds too: How much borrowing is going on, how much competition does Louisiana have for your money? If thirty-year AA-rated bonds are paying 9%, and that's what they're issuing, then that's what they'll pay you.

If you don't want to tie up your money until the bond matures, you can buy short-term bonds, but then your interest will be less. I recently bought some well-rated tax-exempts for a client, and we had the usual choice. If we wanted thirty-year bonds, the New York state agency that was issuing them would pay him an interest rate of $9\frac{7}{8}\%$. They also offered four-year bonds, but on those they would pay him only 5%.

Of course, what he and most of my clients want is the best of both worlds. They want the very limited risk to principal that goes with short-term bonds and the nice high yields offered by long-term bonds.

They also want the safest bonds in the world. Bonds are rated by two main agencies: Standard and Poor's, and Moody's. Moody's is somewhat tougher in its ratings and so is given more credence by professionals. Symbols are slightly different, with AAA the highest rated bond by Standard and Poor's, Aaa the top for Moody's. Although everybody says "Buy me triple A's," in fact they are very rare, especially among tax-exempts.

You can go from the top down to BBB for S&P or Baa for Moody's and still be considering "investment-grade" bonds. In fact, a fiduciary, like a bank handling the money of a trust, may have to buy bonds rated no lower than BBB. As you would expect, the riskier the issuer appears to be, the more they'll have to pay you to lend them the money.

Most people do not want much risk with their bonds. Just the opposite. They can find plenty of risk with their stocks. Bonds, they feel, should be steady and solid and not bring sleepless nights (although we'll see how they certainly can).

I try to work bonds into a client's investment portfolio as part of the balancing of the whole portfolio. Diversification and balance, as noted many times in this book, are two prime objectives. I don't want my clients to have all their money in real estate or all in stocks or all in any one thing. So bonds — fixed-income securities — are very useful.

This is especially so these days with the flexibility and

variety you can find. You can buy units of a tax-exempt bond trust, for example, and get automatic reinvestment of your interest. You can buy "Ginny Maes," Government National Mortgage Agency bonds, which pay you interest and principal on a monthly basis. You can buy zero-coupon bonds, which pay you no interest but increase in value over their lives. Depends on your needs, your tax bracket, the shape of your whole financial plan.

You can also use bonds for clearly targeted goals. You have a child who will be entering college in ten years and you want to start now to build a fund for those expenses. Also, you are very conservative, like many people who say to me, "We don't want to gamble with the kid's money."

You can buy a ten-year bond that will mature when he is starting college, and every year along the way you can take the interest it pays and reinvest it.

As we'll see in Chapter 16, you could invest more aggressively with stocks or a mutual fund, and it might take you less of an investment to pull those tuition fees together. But with bonds, you can erase most of the doubt that the amount you're going to need will be there when you figure on needing it.

So what's wrong with them?

As you might have gathered from the catch in my voice as I've been talking about them, bonds are not perfect.

They offer, first of all, a relatively low return on your money, to my way of thinking, compared to a well-managed stock portfolio. Currently, if you tie up your $15,000 for thirty years, at 9% you will realize $1350 a year tax-free, which is not bad. But if I invest your money in the stock market, I hope to earn 30% to 40% and I expect to hold the stocks for more than a year so federal taxes will be only at a maximum 20% rate. I expect to earn far more in the market than high-yield tax-exempts would bring.

Then there's the problem of what happens if you buy

bonds for a twenty- or thirty-year period but you need cash before that period is up. You have to sell your bonds.

I recently bought someone $30,000 worth of tax-exempts that mature in 2027. This client was concerned that he wouldn't be alive in 2027, which is probably true. He's forty-six today; if he makes it to 2027, he'll be 90. If he dies before the bonds mature, his heirs will inherit them.

But what happens if somewhere along the way, say in the year 2000, he needs to sell these bonds? Today they are good buys, paying 10% tax-free. But maybe on a bleak day in 2000, the entire universe will be in a monetary uproar and interest rates here on the planet Earth will have risen to 18% or 20%.

If the going rate is nearly twice what our bonds are paying, then obviously we will not be able to sell them for their face value or anything like it. When we go into the market-place to sell our bonds, we'll be offered something like 55¢ or 60¢ on the dollar, which means we'll get only $16,500 or $18,000 for the $30,000 face amount of bonds.

Why would people buy them even at a discounted price? If they pay us $18,000 for the $30,000 face amount of bonds, they get a "current return" of 16⅔% (30/18ths of 10%). That's still less than the going rate of 20% that they could get if they bought newly issued bonds. But with our bonds, when they mature they'll receive the face value of $30,000. The appreciation of $12,000 will be taxed at the favorable long-term rate. Could be a good deal for them, certainly a painful one for us and it is one of the true risks of bonds.

It's possible, of course, that interest rates might have dropped by the year 2000. Bonds might be yielding only 8%. In that case, my client would be in very good shape. Instead of having to sell at a discount, he'd be offered a "premium" for his 10% bonds. He gets the cash he needs and a profit on his investment.

All too often, however, what I encounter are those 6%

tax-exempts that people bought fifteen years or so ago and that are down drastically in price.

The silver lining: What to do if your bonds drop

If you bought 6% bonds many years ago and are still holding them during a period when the going rate is 10%, you've got a big paper loss. But all is not lost. There's a way that you can arrange to have Uncle Sam split the misfortune with you. What you do is to swap the bonds.

Bob Davis, a client of mine who is always active in the stock market, owned $25,000 face amount of Puerto Rico Aqueduct and Sewer Authority bonds. They paid 4.2% and would mature in the year 2000. With that 4.2% coupon, Bob's bonds were worth scarcely more than 50¢ on the dollar. But Bob had scored a fairly good gain in the stock market recently and, in his bracket, would have to give 20% of the gain to the federal government.

What we did was to swap Bob's Aqueduct and Sewer bonds. When we sold them, we created a loss of about $12,000. This loss was matched against his capital gain in the stock market and wiped out the tax on that gain altogether. At the same time we bought another $25,000 face amount of bonds, at a comparable discount price, of a different Puerto Rican Authority. Bob was left with approximately the same quality and the same yield on his new bonds and he had saved all of the tax that would have been paid on $12,000 worth of capital gains in the stock market.

Swaps such as this are never absolutely cost-free. You pay something in transaction expenses, and it is possible that your new bond might be a few years longer in term or a fraction less in yield than the bond that you had sold. But by and large, the two bonds should be essentially equal, though not identical.

If you take a capital loss from a bond swap and don't have a capital gain from stocks or from some other transaction to offset against it, the IRS says that you must apply $3000 of your loss, if it's short-term, against $3000 of ordinary income. This is fine if your loss is indeed short-term, but if it's a long-term loss, and that's usually the case when swapping tax-exempt bonds, you must use up $6000 of it against $3000 of ordinary income. Any loss that's left over after the $6000 is used is carried forward for future years' income taxes. But $6000 against $3000 is not a very good bargain, and in general I prefer to use bond swaps against capital gains rather than against ordinary income.

What happens if you've got too good a buy?

For thirty or forty years, up until the start of the 1980s, bond prices dropped. Irregularly and inconsistently, but generally lower. Swapping tax-exempt bonds that were down in price was an annual ritual for some people.

But what if you bought a 13% tax-exempt bond in early 1982? Think about that — locking in such an interest rate for thirty years. Even the 9% and 10% tax-exempts that were available in 1983 look mighty good in comparison with the rates that used to be available.

But bonds can be "called." The issuer may call the bond back from you, giving you $1000 or perhaps $1030 for each $1000 face value of bonds that you hold. Generally an issuer won't try to call bonds unless the market has changed and he is now able to issue new ones with at least a 2% lower interest rate than the ones he is calling in.

However, most bonds offer call protection, which, except for unusual circumstances, guarantees you the ownership of the bond for a specific number of years. Most utilities give five years; some have been issued with seven or ten years. Corporates run to ten years and most tax-exempts go ten years.

Most housing finance bonds have "extraordinary call provisions," which allow the agency that issues them to call them away from you if they are unable to use the money they have raised. Many revenue bonds have "sinking funds," under which some bonds are called away by random lot. This is a way for the issuer to gradually retire his debt, and for you it is a way to play Russian roulette. Let's say you own $25,000 worth of a hospital revenue bond. You might find that your number has come up in the lottery and that five of your twenty-five bonds have to be turned in for cash.

A client of mine, Eddie Candido, got caught in one of the strangest cases I have ever seen where extraordinary call provisions were exercised.

Eddie, referred to me by a friend of his, owned an automobile dealership in Richmond, Virginia, and had seen his share of ups and downs in business and the stock market. I told him that I did not expect any special problems in running his tax-exempt bond portfolio and that I would handle his common stock account the same as I ran any other.

"Lots of luck, Stan," he said. "You put my dough into the same stocks you use for your other clients, and we all lose money. What I buy always goes sour."

As it turned out, he had good results in stocks but a reversal in bonds that seemed to confirm his belief that he was hexed. In his bond portfolio when he came to me were fifty bonds of the Virginia Housing Authority. In late 1982, the VHA had issued $100 million worth of bonds paying 13⅜%. That was an outstanding rate, and Eddie bought fifty of those bonds. The money being raised by the bonds was supposed to back mortgages on one-family houses, but by the time the Authority got the cash, mortgage rates had dropped and they had no use for that very expensive $100 million. Just five months later, they called in the whole issue, took back the bonds and returned the money to some very unhappy investors, including Eddie Candido, who had been looking forward to years and years of 13⅜% interest payments.

With the money he got back, I had to buy for Eddie fifty bonds of another issue at only 9½%. But 9½% was the going rate when we got the money back, and Eddie was stuck with nearly 4% less yield than he originally expected.

Those Housing Authority bonds, like others with extraordinary call provisions, offered an exceptionally high yield. They usually do pay more. But Eddie should have been suspicious of that yield. If he had bought bonds from another agency at that time, he might have gotten 1% or 2% less, but he would have escaped those extraordinary call provisions and been able to benefit from those bonds for years. As it was, the replacement bonds I bought him did provide the usual ten-year call protection.

What happens if you buy Penn Central?

In the years before Penn Central went bankrupt, bond wizards on Wall Street recommended those bonds because they knew the company was "fundamentally sound."

Lockheed? The City of Cleveland? Chrysler? New York City? Saved in one manner or another, but if you tried to sell one of their bonds in the midst of a crisis, you got a terrible price.

If you could wait out the crisis, your nerves would take a beating, but the bond prices would come partway back up. Still, that can be very scary business.

I had a client in 1969 for whom I did a wonderful thing: I sold out his entire stock portfolio at the top of the market. The man had $500,000 in hand, and I started sketching out moves for a nice, neat, intelligently balanced plan for that half-a-million bucks.

"I know what I want to do with the money, Stanley," he

told me soon after. "You don't have to bother with a whole plan. I want to buy tax-exempts."

"You don't mean put all of it into tax-exempts?"

"Yep, that's just what I mean."

"It's your money, Allan, but that's crazy."

"Why crazy? You're the one who's always talking about taxes."

"Yeah, but that doesn't mean you take all your money and buy tax-exempts."

"Stanley, I think you're terrific and you've made me a lot of money. But I've thought this through and if I get the maximum yield, it's going to finance my retirement. Stanley, please, this is what I want to do."

He not only wanted tax-exempts, he wanted the highest yield available — and he didn't much care about risks and ratings.

The highest yields at the time were, God help me, tax-exempts from the great City of New York. He bought $500,000 worth, and for many of the ensuing years, he was absolutely terrified. When New York City finally pulled out of its financial crisis, he calmed down, but by then interest rates were much higher and his bonds were still far down in price.

Now, in the case of New York City, the rating services had reservations, but they didn't rate the bonds nearly as low as they should have. In rating bonds, the services examine the credit history of the community or company and apply all of their financial ratios to measure stability. But it isn't enough to just crunch the numbers. You've got to consider the social and demographic and economic factors that might spell trouble in later years.

My own experience is that the services hardly ever anticipate really catastrophic problems. Instead, we see lots of new bond issues coming out with high ratings, and then when trouble strikes, the ratings get lowered. For example, the bonds of the state of Washington Public Power Supply System nuclear projects 1, 2 and 3 were rated AAA when they were issued. As it became apparent that this whole nuclear power plan was in trouble, that costs were grossly underestimated while the potential market was overestimated, the ratings were lowered to AA, then A1 and finally suspended. WPPSS, or "Whoops" as it is appropriately called, has actually defaulted on $2.5 billion of its bonds. It is the largest default in municipal bond history, and as I write, the whole mess is in the courts and undoubtedly will be there for some time.

Not all triple A's are equal

I cannot duplicate a rating service's scrutiny of some city or company or even power system. But I do try to impose my own kinds of judgments.

A "general obligation" bond, for example, will pay less than a "revenue" bond with the same rating, but I still might buy general obligations.

Often they are less risky. In their fine print you will find the classic phrase "full faith and credit." So if the city of Chicago issues general obligation bonds, all of its resources and tax revenues are behind the bonds. There is some comfort in that, although if you consider what happened to New York City, you can see that the term "general obligation" doesn't automatically mean "safe."

Revenue bonds are issued by a particular agency, say the Little Rock Airport Development Authority, and they back those bonds with the money they raise from their operations. Highway authorities, mortgage-finance agencies, water and sewer authorities all issue these revenue bonds.

As I've said, I try to make judgments that go beyond a ledger sheet. I try to get a sense of long-range social and demographic trends and how they'll affect the bonds I'm considering. What are you buying if you lend money to a large city with large problems and political pressures that keep leaders from being able to do much about those problems? What are you buying if you lend money to a large blue chip company in a declining industry and you lend it for thirty years? Many of the most harrowing bond experiences, after all, have come from blue chip companies.

What are you buying if you lend money to an industry in political turmoil? Once upon a time, public utilities were the darlings of bond buyers. They reasoned that the things were monopolies and that it was unlikely that, say, Commonwealth Edison would go out of business because the city of Chicago would always need electricity and Commonwealth Edison was the only supplier.

Now a number of utilities find themselves at war with consumers, politicians and environmentalists. Con Edison is not allowed to build a pumped storage plant on the Hudson River. The Shoreham nuclear power plant on Long Island gets built, but then the utility is informed that the plant may not be used because there might be a nuclear accident and nobody has yet figured out what to do with all the inhabitants of Long Island if that happens. Or Three Mile Island nearly melts down and the whole nuclear power business is threatened.

The appeal of bond trusts

A bond trust, tax-exempt or otherwise, can cut some of your risk in bonds and do away with the problem of what to select.

When you buy units of a bond trust, you're buying an instant portfolio, fifteen, twenty, twenty-five different bonds that the trust holds.

That kind of diversification is one protection, but if you buy a trust, be sure that there is variety in its selection. If it has nineteen bonds, but six of them are issued by the same state agency and nine of them are hospital and nursing home bonds, you don't have real diversification.

Trusts usually select only A or better-rated bonds, and they'll spell out for you just what the ratings are for each bond in their portfolio.

There are also insured bond trusts. All the bonds in a trust's portfolio might be single A's, but if the trust as a whole has insurance, it will be AAA-rated. With insurance, you'll receive a slightly lower yield, maybe 0.3% less, because the trust has to pay for the insurance. But if one of the bond issuers in your trust's portfolio fails to pay interest when it's due, the insurers will make good. And if an issuer actually goes bankrupt, the insurance will pay you.

There is a 4% to 4½% load, or fee, when you buy these trusts, and they are issued in units of approximately $1000 each. They are growing in popularity and well worth considering. They have one additional feature that may appeal to you: They will automatically take your interest income and reinvest it, buying new bonds to do so. If you really don't need that income currently, this gives you a convenient way to compound it. But beware: You know exactly what interest rate you'll get on the trust units when you buy them, but you have no control over the rate that the reinvestment account will get, and it will vary.

I have seen many people buy tax-exempt bonds year after year and spend the interest the bonds yield year after year. True, they build up a portfolio of tax-exempts, and at the end of twenty years, buying regularly at the rate of $10,000 a year, they have a portfolio worth $200,000. And each year the interest from bonds increases from, say, $1000 the first year to about $20,000 the twentieth year, if we assume the bonds are paying at the rate of 10%. Which means that these people have $20,000 of interest income by the twentieth year. And beyond that, they have $200,000 worth of bonds to take into retirement, which will continue to pay them $20,000 a year, again tax-free.

But look at what might have been if they had reinvested the interest income. Investing the same $10,000 a year and keeping their hands off the interest for twenty years, they would, assuming a 10% rate, end up with more than $600,000 in that retirement fund, and 600 bonds would pay them $60,-000 a year tax-free. Three times as many bonds and three times the income.

Treasuries, the ultimate triple A's

Complete safety freaks love Treasuries. If you lend money to the federal government, you do have the highest level of safety bonds can provide. They are even safer than a bank account. Your Treasury bill, note or bond is a direct obligation of the US government, while your bank account is insured by an agency of the federal government, so a notch below in safety.

More important to an investor, whatever you might earn from a bank deposit is taxable by the Feds, your state and local governments. Whatever you earn on a Treasury bill, note or bond is free of state and local taxes. A state may not tax the federal government. You do, however, have to pay the Feds, so I consider treasuries as taxable bonds and therefore of limited use.

You can find Treasuries for practically any length of time, from three months up to thirty years. They are very liquid, can be bought and sold whenever you want. When you buy a bill, it is issued at a discount and matures at face value. So with your six-month bill, on which the Feds are paying you 8%, you might buy it with around $9600 and it will mature and pay you $10,000.

This feature can be helpful at certain times, usually when I need a short-term investment and my alternative is a money market fund. If I buy six-month bills in July and they mature the following January, all my interest is collected on maturity. So in addition to my exemptions from state and local taxes, I am able to postpone the federal taxes for a full year, until I file my return. With a money market fund, I would have been receiving interest every month, and I'd have to pay all the taxes, national, state and local, by the following April 15.

I can usually live without the ultimate safety of the government, but there are customers who insist on it, sometimes for sound reasons. I had one fellow who had established a prize at a university. He wanted a device that allowed him to fund his gift and forget about it. We bought long-term Treasuries, and both he and the university knew that they could announce the prize (the interest on the Treasuries) with complete confidence that the money would be there to cover it each year.

I also bought Treasuries not long ago for a client with a particular need. He told me that in nine months, he was going to be putting $50,000 into a house. He had a substantial salary and an investment portfolio, and he wanted to be absolutely sure he'd have that cash available.

Treasuries were the best thing for him. I could buy them to mature in the month when he wanted his money, and of course he'd be spared state and local taxes on this income. I couldn't find a tax-exempt note that would do as well for us.

Zero coupon bonds

Fairly new creations, zero coupon bonds pay you no interest at all from the time you buy them until their maturity. In lieu of interest they rise in price. So if you buy a zero coupon bond for $6,000, it might be a fifteen-year bond with a face value of $30,000. That would mean that you would collect the full $30,000 on maturity, and incidentally, these figures work out to a compounded rate of something over $11\frac{1}{2}\%$. You can buy zero coupon bonds with a variety of maturities, and they come both taxable and tax-exempt.

Usually the rate you get on a zero will be slightly less than what you would get on an ordinary bond of comparable quality, but the zero has advantages that compensate. You know exactly what your total rate of return will be if you hold the zero to maturity, as if the interest you might have received along the way had been reinvested at a guaranteed rate. With other bonds, assuming you do reinvest your interest income, you don't know what that'll bring you. Each reinvestment could well pay you a different return.

You can sell zeros before they mature, and depending on the market, you might do well or badly, the same as with any other bond you sell before it matures. If interest rates don't fluctuate while you're holding it, you would expect it to move up steadily toward its maturity value.

I recommend these for clients who don't need the interest earnings over the years, want to build the values of their assets over a long period. They're especially good in tax-advantaged accounts, like retirement plans.

Even though zeros don't pay you any actual interest, if you buy taxable zeros, the IRS will hit you for the tax on the "imputed interest" each year. They figure out that theoretically each year your zero increases in value, and they tax you on that increase. Tax-exempt zeros are not very common, but they allow you to avoid any taxes along the way and take the full value of the zero at maturity in a lump sum, also tax-free.

One important point if you consider zero coupons: Be extra safe. Think about maturity burdens. Let's assume that Company A issues $6 million worth of ordinary bonds maturing in fifteen years and Company B issues $6 million worth of zero coupon bonds. A will have to pay interest every six months for fifteen years and at the end of the fifteen years will have to cough up $6 million to pay off the bond issue. Company B will not have to pay a penny in semiannual interest, but at the end of fifteen years it will need $30 million ready for the bondholders, not $6 million.

When you buy zero coupon bonds, you want to be very certain that the corporation issuing them is going to be alive and well and able, in fifteen years' time, to pony up five times as much money as might be needed on an ordinary bond.

If I were willing to buy an ordinary bond rated single A, I would probably want at least a double-A rating for a zero coupon bond.

CHAPTER 13

*B*eyond stocks and bonds: *Why commodities and futures are not for you, but real estate might be*

YOU'VE HEARD of people reaping medium-sized fortunes overnight or in a week simply by buying and selling pork bellies? So have I. I even understand what it is they did and I still won't try it. I still won't buy a contract for pork bellies, in which I am basically betting that by the time those actual pigs are ready for delivery to the market — oh yes, there are real, live pigs being fattened up here — their value, and so the value of my contract, will go up and I can sell it for a fat profit (excuse the pun).

It is true that enormous profits are made in the commodities market, and it is also true that murderous losses are borne, and for the same reasons: extraordinary volatility and small margin requirements.

Stanley Kroll, one of the more famous commodity traders in recent years who is indeed supposed to have earned millions in a matter of days, called his wife on the last of those days and told her he wanted to meet her for lunch, he had a present for her. He drove up in a Rolls, fresh from the dealer.

Kroll traded for himself as well as for his discretionary accounts, for which he could buy and sell without consulting his clients. He also had some one thousand nondiscretionary customers who ran their own accounts and for whom he was the broker. I don't know how many of those discretionary clients were also able to go tooting off in Rollses, but very few of the ones who traded on their own ever made any money at all. Which should give you some idea of how complex and awesomely risky commodities really are.

There is so much about them out of your control. You might find yourself holding copper contracts. You are happy about them because your commodities broker has assured you of the world's ever-increasing need for copper and because you could buy them on margin and have to put down only 15% of their full price. Then you pick up the *Times* and something catches your eye that in other days would slip by. It's a short wire-service dispatch from Ghruhuru, one of those small, newer African nations. Apparently, according to this incomplete story, there has been a coup in Bombuzu, the capital of Ghruhuru.

To almost everybody else reading the *Times* that morning, the story is merely filler, type to take up the space around a handsome ad from Bergdorf's. But it takes your breath away.

When you reach your broker on your first call that morning, he confirms your palpitations. Thanks to the coup, shipments of copper from Ghruhuru, a major producer, will drop to nothing. The price of copper is already soaring. The moral? A coup eight thousand miles away suddenly drops tens of thousands of dollars into your account.

But supposing it wasn't copper the broker had sold you, it was wheat. "The world has to eat," he reminded you. "Everybody needs wheat. Even the Russians."

This time God and nature are not on your side. The weather over the Great Plains turns out to be absolutely perfect for wheat, just the right amount of rain, just the right number of sunny days. The crop is spectacular, exceeding everyone's expectations, and so is the crop in the Ukraine. The Russians are not buying this year, the market is glutted, your wheat contracts tumble.

Maybe you like coffee instead. This time there's a natural catastrophe, only it's in your favor. Down in Colombia there are floods, earthquakes, pestilence and hail. Half the coffee crop is wiped out. Bad for Colombia, good for you. The price of coffee soars. The value of your contracts soars. Of course, if instead Colombia produced its biggest coffee crop in years, and so did Brazil, Jamaica and six African countries, because this time instead of natural disasters all of those nations enjoyed perfect growing conditions, then you are badly hurt.

You are speculating on the future, as in "futures." You speculated that the price of copper or wheat or coffee was going to rise. Most of us are not very good at creating acts of God or coups, yet if your speculation turns out to be wrong, you pay dearly. You might have bought futures in a great variety of things, all equally beyond your control: corn, sugar, gold, silver, cattle, Treasury bills, foreign currencies, our famous pork bellies.

Is there a way of cutting some of those fearful risks? Could you have protected yourself and your coffee contracts? Perhaps, if you made an intensive study of coffee and climatic cycles and the international coffee market and prayed a lot.

The search for protection, in a way, fuels the futures market. That farmer fattening up those pigs is worried about covering all his costs and making some kind of profit. He has months of feeding and caring before his pigs are ready for the slaughterhouse. So he sells a contract on those pigs, agreeing to a set price when he delivers them. He might make a greater profit if he waited, but then again he might not. The futures contract he sells relieves him of certain worries, is his hedge against violent price variations.

In the commodities market, in Kansas City or Chicago or New York, there are players who think that a pig farmer is nothing but a pig farmer. His livestock will be worth more, they say, much more by the time those pigs are delivered in, say, six months. So they buy a pork belly contract on that assumption. And it might be sold again and again, until you buy it.

Theoretically, if you don't sell that contract before its maturity date, you become the owner of a carload of pork bellies, and indeed amateur commodities players have nightmares of the smelly things showing up on their doorsteps. Before that happens, you unload your contract.

When it comes to my clients and their financial plans, I have no use for commodities or futures of any kind. I can't stay on top of those extremely risky markets, so I can't responsibly put clients into them.

Beyond which, those contracts don't lend themselves to planning. They don't last, they expire. You buy that pork belly contract, it has a maturity date on it, usually a matter of months, and you must sell it by then. That kind of thing destabilizes a financial plan. But if I put a client into a piece of real estate, we can decide when it's to our best advantage to sell, if ever.

In a way, buying into a commodities fund, as we'll see, allows you continuity. Even so, I steer clear of the whole market and advise my clients to do so.

Which doesn't mean they always listen to me. Some of them get caught up in the excitement of the big killings, no matter how I warn them.

Last March I had a call from one of my sometime clients who needed, he said, a tax shelter. He had just made $32,000 in the commodities market and was calling to give me plenty of time to shelter his windfall.

"What did you make it in?" I asked.

"I don't know exactly," he replied. "It's a managed account."

He had, in other words, given his money to one of the commodity houses and told them to run it for him, which, if you must play that game, is better than trying to do it your-self.

"Have you closed the account?" I asked. If not, there wasn't much point to any long discussion about a shelter be-cause his $32,000 could go up or down so fast that our con-versation would be an academic waste of time.

"No, it's still open," he replied. "But I'm trying to do what you always told me to do, buy my shelter early in the year."

I sent him two prospectuses and heard nothing for three weeks, when he called again.

"Stanley, I can't quite believe this. My commodity gains are now up to $45,000."

"That's terrific. You look over those shelters?"

"That's why I'm calling, Stanley. I've been so busy, I really haven't had a chance to review them or show them to my accountant. Are they still open? I'm going to need them worse than ever now."

"They're open, you can still get in both of them. But we should move on them. They're both good offerings and they'll be fully subscribed before long."

"I hear you, Stanley, I hear you. I'll get it taken care of right away."

"I gather you've closed that commodities account?"

"Not quite yet," he said.

"So you don't know exactly how much you'll need to shel-ter?"

"I do. I told you, $45,000."

"Phil, my friend, even as we speak that number is changing. I hope for your sake it's changing upward."

The next call came ten days later.

"You'd understand this better than I, Stanley, but the com-modities guy told me that pork bellies had gone soft, and the soybean crop was much better than anyone expected, and a couple of other surprises like that."

"What do you have left?"

"About $20,000. Any advice?"

"I can still get you into one of those shelters. Take your $20,000 and run."

The commodities broker was more convincing. Phil had already breathed deeply of those thin, seductive vapors, witnessed those lightning profits. Don't fold now, the commodities guy told him, we're about to score on wheat.

When Phil had $3000 left in his account, he closed it out. All things considered, he was quite lucky.

Phil had put his money in a managed account, which at least gave him half a chance. A better way to invest in commodities, in my opinion, is through a commodity fund. They work like mutual funds, spreading their investments among a number of commodities and giving you some diversification and balance. Even so, your risks are high and some of these funds have folded.

Adding to all the perils of this kind of investing, there are an unusually large number of con artists working commodities and futures in general. So unless you are prepared to become a complete futures maven, you'd better tread with extreme caution.

A discouraging note on gold, silver and diamonds

Gold is wonderful for fairy tales, James Bond and investment gurus who see the end of western civilization just around the corner.

For the rest of us, it's best forgotten. To begin with, put your money into gold bullion and you have a "nonearning asset," one that doesn't pay you any dividends.

It also costs you money to keep it. There are dealer charges, sales taxes, storage charges and fees for analyzing your gold, assay fees.

I have heard all the claims that gold is a wise investment because it is "countercyclical." Put 10% or 15% of your investments in gold because when stocks drop, this school informs us, your gold will be more valuable than ever. Not always so. In the bear market of 1981–82, the decline in gold was more severe than the drop in common stocks on the New York Stock Exchange.

Investing in silver offers you all of the problems of gold and even greater volatility. The high for silver came early in 1980, when it reached $50.50 an ounce and the Hunt brothers were trying to corner the market. Gold at that point was selling at its all-time high too, $850 an ounce. By June 1982, silver had dropped below $6 an ounce and gold below $400 an ounce.

Rather than buying the precious metals themselves, if you must invest in them, consider buying the stocks. There are gold-mining stocks, such as Homestake in the United States, or Campbell Red Lake in Canada, or the major South African mines, which trade here as American Depository Receipts (ADRs). President Stein, Vaal Reefs and Kloof are among them, and as a group they tend to pay very substantial dividends. There are also mutual funds, such as International Investors, and closed-end trusts, such as ASA, which you can buy on the New York Stock Exchange.

As beautiful as diamonds are, as much joy as they bring to Elizabeth Taylor, they have only one justification as an investment: if you are planning to flee the country.

Allow me a brief quiz on diamonds, which encompasses all of the major arguments I have heard for investing in them.

True or false?

A. DeBeers controls the price and supply of diamonds, so there are no violent fluctuations in price to worry about.

B. The price of diamonds never drops, it only rises and rises steadily.

C. Over the years, diamonds have appreciated in value

more than any other commodity or collectible item and more than the stock market has risen.

D. Diamonds are the only store of value that enable you to hold a million dollars in the palm of your hand.

Of all of the above, only D is correct. If you are planning to flee the country, you can easily carry a million dollars' worth of diamonds in the palm of your hand.

Otherwise diamonds most certainly can drop in price, and rather drastically. In the early spring of 1980, a one-carat, absolutely perfect diamond was supposed to be worth $62,000. By the fall of 1982, it was worth about $16,000.

Another problem with them is what they cost you. For average diamonds, the kind of thing you'll find in an engagement ring, the retail price is nearly twice the wholesale price. Think of that for a moment in terms of your buying an over-the-counter stock from your broker. Yes, I can get that stock for you, he tells you. It's 20 bid, 40 offered. You'll have to pay 40. That $4000 diamond you bought had a wholesale price of something over $2000. Which means that if you buy that diamond today and hold it for ten years, during which time the inflation rate is 7% a year, you will just break even if you sell the diamond at the end of ten years.

In case you're now worried about Richard Burton and that million-dollar beauty he gave Liz, let me ease your concern. At that level the markup is probably more like 10% or 15%.

Real estate is another matter ... maybe

This has been a chapter filled with warnings and discouragements, but real estate is different. I try to blend it into every financial plan, and I try to discourage clients from doing it themselves.

Without expertise in the business, you're going to get hurt buying and managing real estate by yourself. You won't be able to make the critical decisions about location. You won't be able to manage the financing and run the property to make your investment profitable. Real estate is not a passive investment. You don't plunk your money down for an apartment house, sit back and watch it grow.

You do not do what Dr. Lasker and his wife did. Over the years they began spending more and more time in Florida, both as tennis buffs and as caring children. Their parents had retired there, and it was by watching them that the Laskers thought they saw a ripe opportunity. Their parents had bought condominiums for themselves at reasonably good prices, which rose nicely through the early 1970s.

With their accountant assuring them that they could write off most of their Florida trips if they were actively buying real estate down there, the Laskers made more trips, improved their net games and bought five condos.

It took all the investment money they had, and it was incredible to me to hear what they had done when they finally came to me. Of course, by then it was too late. They had bought when the market was softening, although they couldn't perceive that because they didn't know much of anything about the overbuilt Florida condo market. All they knew was that they were able to drive great bargains, as they put it, get all kinds of discounts and concessions.

One of the problems with real estate is the limited amount of information readily available. It's there, but it takes a lot of digging to get it. It's not like buying a stock, where you can get annual reports, write-ups from your broker, charts and analyses in newsletters and magazines.

The Laskers knew little more than what the salesmen and developers had told them. As amateurs, they did not have the techniques, contacts, or the time to gather the solid information they should have had on which to base their investments.

Nevertheless, they bought and then they struck another

problem with real estate — they couldn't sell. Unlike shares of common stock, which you can usually sell in a moment, real estate is not always liquid. At times there are no buyers whatsoever. You are stuck with your properties, with your capital in cement.

That's the state the Laskers were in when they came to me for a financial plan. There was hardly anything I could do with or for them. They had no money to invest.

Eventually they would be able to sell those condos, most likely at a profit. But imagine the cost of having all that money tied up all those years and paying mortgage interest, maintenance charges and other expenses all along the way.

One intelligent alternative for many of my clients is a real estate limited partnership, and here I'm not talking about real estate deals that are primarily tax shelters, as we discussed in Chapter 6. These are real estate investments that are managed for you by a partnership that buys and runs properties to earn rental income and eventually to sell the properties for capital gains.

In these public offerings your risk is limited, and the thing is set up so that benefits pass through to you and the other limited partners.

There are some tax benefits that will pass your way, but the main objectives here are earnings and capital gains.

Ordinarily you buy into these with a single investment, unlike a real estate shelter deal, which you usually must invest in for five or six years. You put up your $10,000 or however much you want, buying into the partnership.

Typically, for the first three to five years of the partnership, you'll receive income and some tax deductions. Maybe in the third year you'll get an income check of $800 and a tax write-off of $550 on your $10,000. Then your write-offs will dry up while your income continues, and part of it is going to be tax-free.

Around the sixth or seventh year, maybe later, the general

partner who organized and managed the deal, will be looking to sell the property for a profit.

There are some large, reputable national companies offering a variety of limited-partnership investments, organizations such as Carlyle-JMB, First Capital, Consolidated Capital, Balcor–American Express, Fox and Carskadon. Their real estate deals are usually varied and spread around the nation, which cuts down your risk.

Sold by brokerage houses, these public offerings bring a further enticement: They are rarely challenged by the IRS.

Checklist for Chapter 13

1. Be extremely cautious when it comes to investing in commodities or futures of any sort. It is true, as you have doubtless heard, that you can make a fortune overnight with them, but you can also be wiped out just as quickly and for the same reasons: They are so volatile and you can buy them on very small margins.

2. Futures often fluctuate in response to acts of God and nature and the most bizarre events over which you have no control or chance of predicting.

3. If you must play the game, carefully consider commodity funds.

4. Gold, silver and diamonds are all beautiful to wear and behold and all are risky as investments.

5. If you must play the precious-metals game, carefully consider buying the stocks of mining companies, mutual funds or closed-end trusts.

6. Real estate can be an excellent investment, but don't try to do it yourself. Selecting and managing real estate properties is a tough profession, not recommended to casual investors.

7. Look instead to a limited-partnership public offering from one of the large national syndicates.

CHAPTER 14

Planning for the worst with zero life insurance

IT IS REMARKABLE the number of people I encounter with life insurance policies that don't do for them what they need, are expensive to maintain and that they never fully understood in the first place.

There is no other "investment" — if I may call it that — that so involves the deepest emotions: fears of death, protection of family, peace of mind. And of course, those are exactly what the half-million insurance salesmen in America understand and play upon.

One of the worst cases I ever encountered was a suspicious, insecure man with a small but very profitable business whose accountant, the only person on earth he trusted, was also an insurance broker. The accountant sold him one policy after another while shooting down every other investment possibility brought to the businessman.

When Lieffer came to me for some advice on investments for his company's pension plan, I began to open his can of worms and was astonished. First I discovered that the accountant was also something of a tipster on cheap stocks and had convinced Lieffer to dump a big chunk of the pension plan's money into a very speculative over-the-counter stock, a move that had cost the fund about $95,000.

Then, as I questioned him a bit about his own resources, I found several million in life insurance and not a blessed other thing.

When I told him I had never encountered a situation quite like his, he told me not to worry about his personal affairs, all he wanted was guidance on the pension's investments. Yet after a bit of discussion, the two inevitably became intertwined. The accountant was responsible for the costly investment, the same wizard who had put Lieffer into that obscene amount of life insurance. The connection and the point, I thought, were obvious.

"If you want a certain amount of life insurance, fine," I told him. "But a man like you should be investing in several other things as well."

"Let me think about it," he answered, a reply that I have come to realize means, "I can't face that."

Sometimes the attachment to life insurance is rather touching, even though it's still not very sound. One client in good health and with considerable insurance took out another $250,000 on himself after his wife underwent a mastectomy. There was no logic in his move. If there was a danger of anyone dying, it was his wife. Yet he somehow thought the gesture would comfort her, give her a greater sense of protection.

Which is not to say that there are no uses for life insurance. As I have said, I am also an insurance broker. But my approach to my product is quite different from the approaches of other salesmen. It's built around five of my own laws.

1. Only insure when you have an insurable interest, or when the loss of someone is going to have a financial effect on the lives of others.

2. Never mix insurance with investments. Go for insurance and pure insurance, if that's what you need, and get as much for your dollar as you can. It is, as we'll see, the basic argument for buying term insurance rather than whole life insurance.

3. Adjust the amount of insurance you carry to your changing needs.

4. Self-insure as much as possible, cover only catastrophic losses.

5. Aim for zero insurance by building up your other assets to the point where they can serve all your insurance needs.

Let's consider each of these principles.

Only insure when you have an insurable interest

John Duncan believed in life insurance. His father had died when John was eight years old, and his memories of the financial effects of the death are seared in his mind.

Before the man's death, the family was living comfortably in an upper-middle-class suburban Chicago neighborhood, happy and ostensibly protected from the worst of life. John's father was succeeding as a lawyer, was in good health and carried no life insurance. It was always something he intended to look into and never did. His law firm offered no insurance plan, either, which was not uncommon in those days.

John and his mother and younger sister were forced to move not long after the death and to change their lives completely. For a while they lived with his grandparents, finally found an apartment they could afford not too far away. They had to be near his grandparents because for the first time in her life his mother had taken a job, as a saleswoman in a downtown department store. She was still working when John and his sister got home from school, and there were no day-care centers then. John's grandmother filled in until his mother came home for dinner.

The family had certainly survived, and John had become a lawyer like his father, putting himself through college and law school with scholarships and part-time jobs.

When we first reviewed his affairs, he was carrying $1

million of whole life insurance on himself and paying a staggering $12,000 in annual premiums, with an additional $200,000 policy on his wife and $100,000 on each of his children, aged two and four.

When I told him I thought that was an excessive amount of insurance, he told me about the trauma of his father's death and how that was never going to happen to his family.

I certainly understood, but still I had to ask him why he had decided to insure everyone in the family and how he had come up with the amounts he had.

That, he explained, had all been worked out carefully with his life insurance salesman.

There was no question that he needed insurance, I said, but I was troubled by his present plan.

"First of all," I said, "the matter of who needs it: Your wife is not now working, so all of the family's income depends on you. Obviously you have to be insured. For how much, we can consider in a moment."

He told me that his wife planned to return to work when the kids were ten and twelve, and that that had nothing to do with whether he was alive and well at that time, earning a million bucks a year, or any other consideration. She had worked and intended to return to it after giving the kids what she considered enough full-time mothering.

At present, though, as I pointed out to John, she earned nothing. If she were to die, there would be no loss of income. John would need some kind of housekeeper, probably living with them, to look after the children, and he might need additional help as well. In that sense he had an insurable interest in his wife.

How much? Did he need the $200,000 policy he was presently carrying? Probably not, since that money, conservatively invested in a tax-free bond trust, would bring him something like 8.5%, or $17,000 a year. In all likelihood he wouldn't need that much to cover his new household expenses.

If his wife was working, then I'd want insurance to cover the loss of her income. In that case John would have an insurable interest in her going beyond the extra help he'd expect to hire.

So we were left with a plan that might diminish the amount of his wife's insurance, eliminate completely the insurance on the kids and leave him carrying the bulk of it.

I knew well enough how his insurance agent had pushed John's coverage up to $1 million: by playing over and over on the theme of "leave your wife without a care in the world, spare her your mother's fate." But what would his wife actually need, if John died, to live just the way she had been living? To be able to keep the house they now had and to stick with her plan of not working until the children were ten and twelve, eight years from now?

There is a way to quantify the amount of insurance you actually need. With John, who was earning $105,000 a year, we sketched out a budget and saw that he and his family spent about $50,000 a year to live the way they now did.

Looking ahead, we wanted to factor in inflation and to figure that if John died tomorrow, his wife still wished to remain a full-time mother for eight years.

What we were talking about was a policy that would yield about $70,000 a year for those eight years. Her financial needs would not disappear at that point, but there were other things we could do with other parts of John's assets to plan for that. The immediate need of the life insurance was to provide that much income for that number of years.

Although the total amount came to $560,000, we were not talking about a policy worth all of that. Rather, we looked at this as if it were an annuity, paying out the $70,000 we required each year while the balance of the money was compounding and earning interest. (We'll examine annuities and life annuity plans in Chapter 16.)

I could show John that what he needed was a $300,000 policy, not the million-dollar beauty he now had.

I also pointed out to him that if we set the plan up this way, it would work only if his wife was willing to make a firm commitment to it. She would have to stick to her plan to return to work at the end of eight years because by then the insurance money would have run out. (In practice, we would be receiving a lump sum of $300,000 from the insurance company and investing it in an "immediate annuity," which is one that makes payments to us immediately upon being set up. We'd draw the $70,000 a year from it we needed, and much of that would be tax-free.)

John reviewed all my numbers, checked the tables. "If we do this," he finally said, "I don't think there's any question about Doris sticking to the plan. If anything, I think she'd want to get back to work all the more. So it isn't Doris who would have any problem with this. It's me."

"How so?" I asked.

"I simply can't feel comfortable with that little life insurance," he replied. "I can follow all your figures, but I still want more." He shrugged. "I told you about my father."

"No problem," I told him. "I'm an insurance broker. How much can I sell you?"

"Supposing I had $500,000?" he asked tentatively. "That seems like a pretty good compromise. Half of what I'm carrying now, but more than you say I need."

"Fine," I said. "But just give me a chance to sell you term insurance instead of the whole life you've got. I really don't want to steal your money."

Never mix insurance with investments:
Term versus whole life

John Duncan's life insurance agent, like his colleagues, made much of the fact that whole life insurance not only provided for his wife and family on John's death, it also offered John something while he was alive. Of the premiums John paid, a portion went for the life insurance, a portion for savings or investment. That second part, the cash value, increased year after year — in the case of John's particular policy, at the rate of 5% a year.

At any time John could borrow all or part of that cash value, take the money tax-free. If he chose not to pay it back to the insurance company, he didn't have to. He would have to pay them interest on the amount borrowed, only 4½% in his case, and until he did pay the full amount back, that amount would be subtracted from the life insurance coverage remaining in the policy.

That was supposed to be the best of both worlds. As I explained to John, to my mind it was just the opposite.

"We've figured out how much insurance you really need," I told him, "and you added on to that. We're talking about coverage of $500,000. Fine, let's get you that and not get it all confused with investments. You want to know that if you die, your wife, Doris, will receive $500,000. That's what you want the insurance policy for, not to have a fund you can borrow against if you need cash. Besides, what the insurance company is offering you for the investment side of the policy absolutely stinks. A return of 5% is disgraceful. I can get you more than 5% in my sleep."

The solution for him and practically everyone is term insurance. Term is pure insurance. No investment, no cash-surrender value, no feebly growing fund you can borrow against. You buy it for a year, five years, for a set term, not for life. Simple insurance, and since it is simple and the agent's commission is much lower, the premium is much, much lower.

In John's case, he could have the $500,000 policy for a current year's premium of a bit more than $500. The same amount of coverage in an ordinary life policy could cost him about $7000. (Depending on how much shopping around he did for the whole life, his premium could vary between $3300 and $7400 for the exact same coverage. That's the nature of the life insurance game. The same policy with two different companies can have one premium that is 100% more expensive than the other.)

A life insurance salesman would argue, of course, that the premium on John's term policy would increase year after year, while the premium on the whole life policy never increased; it would be the same in thirty years as it was the day he took it out. And besides that, he would say, they won't sell you term insurance after you are seventy-five years old. So just when you'll need insurance most, just when you'll be most preoccupied about caring for your loved ones if you die, they'll leave you high and dry.

True, but . . . The premiums on your term policy will increase year after year, but it will take years and years before they are equal to what you have been paying year after year after year to the whole life insurance company.

And instead of giving them all that money, you can invest it, even most conservatively, and create assets that will be greater than the face value of that whole life policy. Those assets will protect your loved ones just as much as a check from an insurance company.

So far as continuing lifelong coverage is concerned, also true, but . . . At present, you pretty much can't buy term insurance after you're seventy-five, but once again, if you have been investing, say, $5000 a year that you'd otherwise use for insurance premiums on a $200,000 policy, when you reach age seventy-five, surely you'll have assets of more than $200,-000.

Term insurance advocates have a slogan: Buy term and invest the difference. It's more than a slogan.

Deposit term, a nice variation. Despite my arguments, I've had clients who still have problems accepting the fact that their premiums will increase each year with term insurance. "Deposit term" is one way of soothing them.

In one situation I was called by an old client, an internist in Philadelphia, whose son-in-law wanted guidance. The young man, in his residency at Hahnemann Hospital in Philadelphia, had made a major study of life insurance plans, and he was terribly confused. He had undertaken the venture the week after he and his wife learned that she was pregnant. It was time for him to buy life insurance, he decided, but which kind?

By the time I spoke to him, he had ruled out whole life. Ordinary life was too expensive, and twenty-pay and thirty-pay life even more expensive. (With those, instead of paying the premiums until you die, you pay for twenty years or thirty years and the whole thing is paid up. But each of those premiums is enormous.)

Term insurance appealed to him, but looking at his resident's salary, he didn't like the idea of those yearly increases.

Since he felt that way, we bought a deposit term policy, even though I had some reservations. For coverage of $200,-000, his premium was about $700. That was more than he would have paid on a regular term policy for the same amount, but he was willing to pay it. (One of my reservations.) He was also willing to deposit with the insurance company $2000. Because then his premiums would be the same for ten years.

At the end of ten years, the insurance company would return his $2000 deposit and an additional $2000 as well, and his gain would be tax-free. (The amount insurance companies pay on these deposits varies, but it almost always at least doubles your money.)

He would have $200,000 term coverage for ten years, with the premium rate fixed at $700. However, if he dropped the policy before the ten years were up, he'd lose his $2000 deposit. That, according to the insurance companies, covers their expenses of the early years, the cost of the initial physical, the commission, administrative expenses, and so on.

If he wanted to continue the coverage after ten years, he could without another physical. His premiums for the next stretch would be higher, of course, because he would be ten years older.

Some whole life exceptions. There are a few situations with my clients where I do include some whole life insurance in their plans.

One is when we face an estate tax problem. I had a wealthy client whose wife had died, and he was planning to leave everything to his children. If he had been leaving it to his wife, no taxes. But to the kids, he faced heavy taxes.

His solution was to buy enough life insurance to cover the estate taxes. I said, "Let's not buy all that life insurance. Instead, let's take the money those premiums would cost, invest it and then we'll have more than enough for the estate taxes." He felt his way was guaranteed and mine wasn't, and that was true. Also, he wanted whole life, not term. His health was good and he came from a family where everyone lived forever. He feared that with term insurance the policy might become too costly or unrenewable. As noted, most term policies are not available to people over seventy-five. So we bought the whole life insurance. I still think my way was better, but I don't argue much with clients over this one.

Another situation is a "buy-sell agreement," with life insurance to cover the death of a partner in a business. A typical case I had involved two partners in a box factory. One man was the outside representative and supersalesman, the other ran the plant. It was clear that the death of either meant a whole restructuring of the business. And that the dead partner's widow, who would be receiving his 50% of the business, would be wanting money, not an active partner's role in the place.

We evaluated the business at $1 million and had the company buy life insurance on each partner for $500,000. In a separate agreement, the partners affirmed that when one died his wife received $500,000, which represented half the value of the business. The surviving partner then owned the business solely and completely. The widow would get the cash, which she would need, and the surviving partner would get the company, which he would want.

Group life policies. On a broader scale, there is one form of life insurance I normally recommend to all my clients: group life. It is often the best and cheapest deal in life insurance, and when it is, I urge clients to buy as much as their company allows. Usually the company provides them with a term policy as one of the company's benefits and then offers them the chance to buy a limited additional amount at the low group rate. Buy it, I tell them all, with one caveat: Double-check the cost of the group insurance being offered you. Some companies and organizations offer plans that are not such bargains. Compare what you are being offered with the cost of the best available term policy you could buy as an individual.

One problem with group is that it usually lapses before you die. Most people live on into retirement. Yet when you leave the company, you usually lose the group coverage. If you go earlier, obviously you leave that employee benefit behind.

A small number of companies also have group policies designed to stretch through postretirement years. With these, "retired-lives reserves policies," the premiums are higher. The insurance company has figured out how much to charge the company to cover its employees while they are working there and after they retire.

I would hope that by retirement you have other assets that will more than compensate for the loss of the group insurance. I recently sketched out a scenario for a forty-year-old man, an already successful MBA with only promise before him.

We were evolving a plan for him, trying to look ahead. His company gave him $100,000 worth of group insurance, he carried another $50,000 himself. He was, however, thinking of moving to a competitor.

I was sure they would offer him a comparable insurance program, perhaps more. And while there was no telling how long he'd be with them, whether he would stay until he retired or move around some more, at retirement age he was going to have a substantial pension, an IRA, social security, plus all his assets, which we were going to be nurturing for twenty-five years. Forgetting any insurance plan, he and his wife would have plenty to live on by the time he retired and obviously, if he were to die, more than enough for her alone.

Beware of extras. In those cases where we end up buying whole life for my clients, I am firm about avoiding embellishments.

Double indemnity, for example, violates my basic rules. If we decide that you need $500,000 worth of coverage to handle the financial needs you will leave behind, how do those needs change because you get run over by a truck? Why would your wife or husband need twice as much money to cope then as they would receive if you died in your sleep? Why pay the insurance company for such a bizarre option?

Similarly, something like flight insurance is unnecessary. If you have the coverage you need, you should not be paying for more than that.

Beware of "split-funded" insurance plans. In recent years, insurance companies have campaigned heavily among small and medium-sized companies, peddling another plan that's supposed to be the best of both worlds.

This one is the "split-funded" plan for retirement programs. In theory, the insurance company divides the money you and your employees are putting into your retirement plan, assigning part of it to life insurance and part to investments. Everybody owns a share according to his salary level, the number of years he has been putting money into the plan and so on.

It doesn't work. The investment return on these schemes is so bad, I can beat it with any other kind of investment. In fact, I have shot down a number of these things which clients have brought to me and which they were considering for their own companies.

Depending on their circumstances, I have sometimes convinced them that they would be better off buying themselves a term policy outside the retirement program, one they would pay for themselves, or I have set up group life plans and taken the retirement-plan money and invested it.

Whatever solution I propose, I can show them through simple arithmetic that we can always outperform the split-funded plan. Another example of how you lose if you try to mix investing and life insurance.

If you're holding whole life policies, but I've convinced you not to. Take your money and run.

The insurance people hardly had this in mind when they built cash value into their whole life policies, but my advice is to take advantage of that feature, cash in the policy.

Frequently I move clients out of their whole life policy and into term. Of course, I always make sure first that they can do it, that they qualify for term. They take the physical exam and have the term policy issued to them before we allow the whole life policy to lapse.

I ended up doing that with John Duncan and all his insurance. On a far lower scale, I did it recently for the Mathewsons, a couple with no children and really, given their other assets, no need for life insurance at all. They couldn't accept that idea completely, however, so we designed a compromise.

They had about $18,000 cash value in their $100,000 whole life policy. We drew it out and surrendered the policy, and we bought term insurance, also for a total of $100,000. Again, only because they were nervous without it. However, they did concede that in the context of the whole plan I worked out they could safely drop even the term policy in five years.

The premium on the term was about $1400 the first year. And as with all term policies — as whole life salesmen happily remind you — that premium amount increases as you get older. With whole life, of course, your premium is steady and unchanging year after year.

We took the $18,000 they got from their policy and they added $2000 to it. With the $20,000 we bought some tax-exempt bonds paying 9% a year, or $1800 free of taxes. That income more than paid their term insurance premiums for each of the five years they wanted the policy. It was a can't-lose situation.

An interesting footnote to the loan or cash-surrender value in a whole life policy: When you die, it disappears.

Let's say you've had a $100,000 policy for years and years and have finally accumulated $24,000 in it as your cash-surrender value. Then you die. Your grieving widow receives a welcome check for $100,000 from the insurance company. But what happens to the $24,000? The so-called investment side of your policy? Ask the next person who tries to sell you a whole life policy.

Adjust the amount of insurance you carry to your changing needs

Another of my basic insurance rules and another of my problems with whole life.

One of the great selling points of whole life is that if you buy it, keep up the payments, you and yours are covered for life.

People get lulled by such security. It may be that the insurance is constant, while their actual needs are not.

This is especially so in a family with children. While the kids are growing up, whether one or both parents are working, the kids have to be protected from the financial loss of their parents. But the amount of protection they need varies.

With John Duncan, we saw one fairly common situation: His wife had voluntarily stopped working for a while to be a full-time mother. Her intention was to return to work when her children were ten and twelve. Whatever income she would be bringing into the home at that time could affect the amount of insurance her husband might need to carry on himself.

Even if there were no such plan, if John were going to be the sole provider for the entire family, their financial picture would not be static.

For one thing, presumably John would be earning more as the years went by, and we'd be building his assets, increasing his net worth. In that case, if he cut his insurance down, there would still be enough in assets to care for his family.

Further, at some point those two kids of his will grow up. What sort of financial protection will they need when they are in college? Or finish college? He was carrying, you might recall, $1 million of whole life. Forgetting the fact that it was an excessive amount to start with, how much would John need when his kids were able to take care of themselves?

A term policy would give him complete flexibility. We decided that he'd shift from the $1 million whole life policy to a $500,000 term. But even as we were doing it, we were making other calculations with his financial plan, projecting into the years ahead. For a number of reasons I could see the day when he would need zero life insurance.

Especially with John, given his childhood, we would approach that zero point gradually. Again, the essence of term: You are locked into a specific amount of insurance only for one year. Want to decrease the next year? Renew that much less. Or, finally, let the whole thing lapse. As simple and flexible as that.

Self-insure as much as possible, cover only catastrophic losses

Although this rule of mine applies to life insurance, more commonly it is something to use with other kinds of insurance.

Forget minor losses. They are not worth the premiums you'll have to pay. If your house loses a few shingles, you can handle the repair costs yourself. But if someone slips on the ice in front of your house, is crippled and sues you for seven figures, that's when you want insurance.

Same with car insurance. People complain to me all the time that they dented their fender, had to pay $300 to get it straightened out, and their policy had a $500 deductible. They didn't collect a penny.

An intelligent approach to such insurance calls for the largest deductible the company will allow. It's not fenders you have to worry about, it's the horrendous accident. Even then I'm not concerned with car damage. I'm concerned that you kill somebody in such an accident and that person's survivors sue you for millions. Even if you total your car, have to replace it completely. No one likes to drop $10,000 or $15,000, but that is nothing compared with a multimillion-dollar lawsuit.

If you try to insure for every small loss, the odds are terribly against you and in favor of the insurance company. The amount you'll pay in premiums over the years will far outweigh your occasional reimbursement.

The same principles of big deductible and keeping your eye on the big loss are essential to insurance for your home. You are, after all, protecting one of your major assets. A fire, a flood, can level your place. Most home-owner policies will cover you for the home and its contents. You want to collect whatever it will take to replace everything, which usually means that you must insure for at least 80% of the full value. And bear in mind that inflation can affect the value of your belongings. If you bought a policy five years ago, you might want to increase your coverage today. It's going to cost you that much more to replace everything. If you're going to be replacing great works of art and antiques, you might well need more protection than the regular home-owner's policy offers.

You might also supplement your policy for personal liability if you are an attractive target for people to sue. Many of my clients carry umbrella personal liability policies, usually for $1 million, and these policies start paying after the coverage from their home and auto liability insurance has been exceeded. This is very inexpensive insurance.

Disability insurance is wise if like most people you're dependent on a fairly substantial paycheck and if, when it stops coming, you know that such supplements as Workmen's Compensation or Supplementary Security Income from Social Security are not going to be nearly enough. Once again, the higher your deductible, the better. That would mean a policy that would start paying you, say, ninety days after you're disabled rather than thirty days. You should have enough money available to live for ninety days or your financial planning is truly deficient. If you buy the thirty-day payment policy, you'll pay the company a fortune. I recently looked at one that started payments in thirty days; its annual premium was $1500. For one whose payments began after ninety days, the premium was about $500.

Aim for zero insurance

This is where I try to establish all of my clients, at a point where we have built their assets sufficiently so that they and their families are covered and they don't need any more life insurance of any kind.

To be sure, there are times when their assets are high, yet we still maintain whole life and pay the premiums. A client of mine, for example, is seventy-four, has already had one heart attack, and he's been carrying $100,000 of whole life on himself since he was thirty-seven years old. Obviously I couldn't suggest to him that he cash in his policy, even though his wife would have more than enough from his estate without the insurance company's $100,000 check. Why toss away that check?

Other clients with less of an estate who have been carrying whole life for decades must also maintain the insurance because it is significant to the estate and at this point in their lives cannot be replaced.

When a couple comes to me in their early forties and inevitably says, "We've got to have insurance" — often picking a figure like $250,000 out of the air — I make my case for a rational approach to the stuff. But my greater objective is to work with them so that in ten or fifteen years they have enough assets that if one of them dies the other is taken care of.

When they are sixty, they should be able to say, after twenty years of accumulating and investing, "We have a $100,000 stock portfolio and $200,000 in tax-exempt bonds, as well as some property, pension plans and Social Security. In fact, if one of us dies, the other could continue to live just the way we have been living on the income from all this, or maybe with a little help by dipping into the pot. So, obviously, we don't have to be supporting the insurance company any longer."

At that point they have the best insurance of all: self-insurance. Provides for everything, and the premiums are extremely reasonable.

Checklist for Chapter 14

Here are my five rules for life insurance.

1. Only buy insurance when you have an insurable interest, when the loss of someone is going to have a financial effect on the lives of others.

2. Never mix insurance with investments. Go for insurance and pure insurance, if that's what you need, and get as much for your dollar as you can. The investment side of whole life insurance dissipates the amount of insurance your dollar buys, and it is a dreadful investment besides. This is a basic argument for buying term insurance rather than whole life.

3. Adjust the amount of insurance you carry to your changing needs.

4. Self-insure as much as possible, cover only catastrophic losses.

5. Aim for zero insurance by building up your other assets to the point where they can serve all your insurance needs.

CHAPTER 15

Taking care of your kids

WHEN MARK DALEY called from Washington, he said his friend Benton, my editor client, had ordered him to do so. He needed help, Daley told me, but he didn't want a whole financial plan.

"Do you do kids?" he asked.

"Kids?"

"I don't want the whole menu," he said. "I just want to figure out some way to put my kids through college."

Normally I don't do parts of a plan, but since he came from Benton, I asked him, "How old are they?" I wanted to see how much time there was, how difficult it would be to build a fund. People who call me with such a single-minded concern usually call when their kids are only a few years away from college and they realize they'd better do something about paying for it. There is always a way, even if there are only two or three years of investing time before college starts. But the earlier, the better and the easier.

"Mark Junior is nine. His sister, Vanessa, seven."

There was plenty of time. I told him I could see him at the end of that month, when I would be in Washington, but only if he understood that I couldn't create a plan for his kids in the abstract. What we did for his kids would depend on the financial circumstances of him and his wife. So basically I'd have to approach this as if I were developing a whole financial plan for them. They'd have to provide me with all of their data.

"Couldn't you just tell us, 'Invest $5000 in this and $5000 in that, store it in a safe place and repeat every two years'?" he asked.

"A simple prescription?" I said. "I could. But it wouldn't be very responsible. Giving money to your kids is fraught with tax questions. If I hand you a simple prescription, I could lose you thousands of dollars in taxes."

"I was afraid of that," he replied.

Frankly, if he hadn't been a friend of Benton's, I wouldn't have bothered. He conveyed a certain reluctance, and I wasn't terribly eager to spend time convincing him of anything.

I called Benton and told him I was willing to try to help Daley, since he was a friend.

"But I have to ask you: What's he so scared of?"

"He got burned once by one of your brethren," Benton told me. "Guy sold him stocks, insurance, shelters, stuff I never heard of. Called himself a financial planner, just like you, Stanley. Cost poor Mark a lot of dough and a lot of ego. I mean, he survived okay, but he's scared of you guys. I told him at lunch the other day that he had to do something for his kids. I'm paying for Donnie at Harvard right now, as you well know. If we hadn't done some planning for this great day, where the hell would I find $50,000? Wrong school for him anyway, but that's another story."

When I met Mark and Charlotte Daley in their home, a not-quite-renovated house near DuPont Circle, I made the point quickly that they didn't have to buy a thing. I told them that Benton had informed me that their previous experience with a planner had not been a happy one.

"Disastrous," Mark said.

"Why do you want to take a chance with me?" I asked.

"To begin with," Mark said, "Charlotte has been after me forever to start some kind of fund for the kids. Then Benton landed on me for the same thing. He thinks very highly of you, and I'd trust him with my life."

Mark had worked for Benton at one time as a political

reporter. For the last six years he had been with a pollster and campaign consultant. His income varied, rising in election years to about $70,000, dropping in off years to $50,000. His wife had been a reporter also, for a newspaper in Columbus, Ohio, and moved some years ago to Washington with the staff of an Ohio senator. She was now on the regular staff of the Senate Foreign Relations Committee and earned $35,000.

They were extremely engaging people, as you might expect, yet for all their political sophistication, they knew little about taxes as they affected their own situation. And, as usual, taxes make the world of kid-planning go round, whether the idea is to plan for college education, as it commonly is, or for any other reason.

The basic principle, I explained to them, was to shift income away from themselves and their own high tax bracket over to their children, who earned nothing now and would pay taxes only on what their funds earned, which would be at very low rates.

And best of all, the tax law was set up to encourage parents to do just that.

The Daleys' income varied according to election years and Mark's earnings. But I told them to think of themselves as in the 42% bracket at least. If they bought $50,000 worth of bonds and the bonds paid them 10% interest, they'd collect $5000 a year and pay the federal government $2100 of that in taxes. They would come away with $2900.

If, however, they took the same $50,000 and put it into the same bonds in, say, Mark Junior's name, whether in the form of a trust or a "custodial account," the results would be very different. The boy would collect the 10%, or $5000 a year, but his taxes would be more like $500. He'd get to keep $4500.

"The principle is fine," Charlotte said. "But I think you flatter us if you talk in terms of $50,000 worth of bonds."

"Forget those numbers," I told her. "Setting up a fund for

children is not just for rich folk. The tax law makes it simple for everyone, even with much lower amounts."

The law, as of 1981, says that anyone may make a gift to another person of up to $10,000, and neither the person giving the gift nor the person receiving it will have to pay any gift taxes on it. Doesn't have to be a parent to a child or one relative to another. That gift law applies to anyone. As parents, the Daleys could jointly give up to $20,000 a year to Mark Junior and $20,000 a year to Vanessa. If they gave them more as gifts, there would be taxes, unless they got fancy, as we'll see, with such things as Crown loans or Clifford trusts.

"We don't have to get fancy," Charlotte said. "We can't even get close to the $20,000 limit."

"If we could afford to hand over to our kids $40,000 a year," Mark added, "I don't think we'd be having this conversation at all, Mr. Cohen. I think we'd be so rich that I probably wouldn't have to worry about college years ahead at all. I'd simply write out a check when the time came."

"Or like other rich people, we'd have some omniscient family lawyer and he'd simply do it," Charlotte said. "One day there he'd be, our own Edward Bennett Williams, presenting us with papers to sign, and all this money would suddenly be transferred to little Mark and Vanessa and they'd never have to worry again."

"Nor would we."

"I get the picture," I told them. "But don't despair. I can show you a way to set these kids up so their college educations are covered, and it probably won't cost you more than $5000 a year for each kid to get it off the ground."

They looked at each other.

"Honestly," I said. "But I'm getting a little ahead of myself. Let me try to show you how this thing really works. And then we can figure out what kind of money we'll need, over how many years, and how we might invest it."

The whole process is quite simple, I explained. They make

their gifts and we set up "custodial accounts," of which one or the other of them is the custodian. The gifts are given to the children and they are irrevocable. The Daleys can't change their minds after a few years, say "We're short of cash and need a new kitchen" and help themselves to the money in the fund. (Even though, we'll see, parents try.)

As custodians, they decide what to do with the money. Depending on the investment plan, they set the account up with a bank, or maybe a broker. There are guidelines and restrictions to keep them from making any "imprudent" investments or being excessively risky. Margin accounts are not allowed nor is short-selling. Too much risk involved. All securities must be registered.

Within such regulations, they manage the money. If they call the broker, tell him to sell one hundred shares of IBM from the account and send them the proceeds, he'll do what they tell him. They're the custodians. Same if they call the banker or go in with the passbook and withdraw $500. Nobody questions them.

The law says that the money must be for the child's benefit, but may not be spent for normal living expenses, such as food, shelter, clothing. Custodians might start out with a college fund in mind, then along the way decide that a child isn't going to get into college without a better high school. They pull the money out to pay for a private school.

Or maybe the need has nothing to do with school. Maybe the kid needs braces on his teeth. They pull a few thousand out to do it.

"How does the law know?" Charlotte asked. "Supposing you do take the money out and have your kitchen redone?"

"The law doesn't know, usually, unless there is some terrible family battle — a horrible divorce or something. But by far most people obey the law because they care about their kids. They want these funds to be used for their kids."

There are exceptions, of course. I had a client with a fund

for his daughter that I had nothing to do with, yet he called one day telling me he was worried about it. His daughter was approaching twenty-one.

These custodial funds are set up for minors under the control of the custodian — in this case the father — until the children reach their majority, whatever it is in their state. Here it was twenty-one. Once the children are legally adults, the money is theirs. That's a concern parents have.

A fund of, say, $60,000 has been nurtured over the years with the specific intention of using it to pay for college. But the child becomes an adult overnight, in many states at age eighteen, and decides he or she doesn't want to go to college. The kid might make little sense, perhaps is fighting with his parents and decides to go off on his own, travel around the world. A spiteful adolescent, he wants to upset his parents.

Whatever the personal dynamics, the law says that the money is still his. He might take it and blow it, and that prospect worries many parents.

My client's problem was a bit different. His daughter was doing pretty well at college, but she was living with a guy her father had no use for.

"I invested too much in that account," he told me. "Beyond what her college is going to cost, there's almost $50,000 in that fund. I can't simply turn that money over to her."

"Why not?" I asked. "It's hers. It's been hers since the day you gifted it to her."

"I don't trust that guy."

"Tell her."

"It's hopeless."

This man's solution was to take the money and make it disappear, which was illegal. His daughter never really knew how much was in the account. He told her there was enough for college, maybe a few dollars more. So he took the money. (Before the girl finished college, she broke up with the awful boyfriend.)

I should note that figuring out exactly how much you're

going to need to see your children through college is more an educated guess than anything. There are too many years ahead for exact projections, and we can only estimate increased costs and inflation. I know financial planners who appear to be precise in this area, extrapolating and projecting and coming up with an exact number. It's nonsense. There are too many variables. But, as we'll see, I can come up with a realistic range, and one that we can use in a sound plan.

Part of that plan is moderating the amount invested in your child's fund each year. The law does not require you to put in any set amount. Normally, we start out with the largest gifts in the earliest years, if possible, to have the largest amount of money possible working and compounding over the longest period of time.

If we set a range of some $80,000 to assure a projected diploma from Yale and after six years, say, we are close to our goal with another three years to go before the child is finished with high school, we can simply cut back the amounts of your gifts for those remaining years.

Most of my clients, unlike the worried father, enjoy the idea of "overinvesting." Once the plan is in place and they are accustomed to their annual gift, they prefer to let it build. They consider the possibility of graduate school for their child. The extra money in the fund could go for that. Or perhaps there'll be some money left over to start the son or daughter off in the real world.

When I told the Daleys that planning for their children would not be precise, they were actually somewhat relieved. The planner who had bruised them years before had been a big printout man. He did give them exact figures for their then babies, but fortunately they never got around to implementing that part of the financial plan.

To start, I asked them where they would send their kids if they were doing so tomorrow.

"An actual college?" Mark asked.

"If you can," I replied.

"That's very tough," Charlotte said. "I mean, we've talked about schools, but in an unreal way. Mark went to Dartmouth and has always felt it would be nice if Mark Junior went there."

"At the same time," Mark added, "I know there are plenty of other good schools, and who can tell in nine years if he'll be able to get into Dartmouth or be interested? He might prefer some big-city school. Or someplace in a completely different part of the country."

"I went to Ohio State," Charlotte said. "I got a fair education. I want better for Vanessa. But how could I pick, say, Stanford or Brown or wherever now, and make any sense? She's got eleven years before she goes to college."

"Okay," I told them. "These are some of the variables. These are some reasons why we can only start with guesses. In terms of costs and how much we'll need, obviously there's a great difference between a state school and an Ivy League school."

Still, it was clear from what they said in a brief discussion that they were thinking of the best private colleges for their children, and the best are the most expensive. We could begin to calculate, and I did it all with them and my simple pocket calculator.

"Let's take Mark Junior and say he's headed for an Ivy League school that currently costs $10,000 a year. Let's also say that we're going to see an average rate of inflation of 7% for the next nine years, until he's ready to enter Old Ivy. We simply punch out on the calculator 1.07 times $10,000 and hit the equal sign nine times for those nine years." Which is what I did. We went up to $10,700, then $11,449 and so on until in the ninth year we came up with the figure $18,385.

"And that is a fair guess at what little Mark's first year of college will cost you," I told them.

Mark laughed. "That used to be a pretty good annual salary."

"If that number amuses you," I said, "let me punch this two more times so we get into his third year." I came up with $21,048 and multiplied it by four. "We're talking $84,000 for Mark's diploma."

"This is crazy," Charlotte said, "absolutely crazy. More than $160,000 to have the two kids educated?"

"I didn't bring you this far to leave you in pain and hopelessness," I told them. "Stay with me."

Charlotte smiled slightly, but shook her head. "Impossible," she said softly.

"Let's make some other assumptions," I told them. "Let's suppose that you give each child $10,000 a year as a gift."

Together they howled. "Twenty thousand a year . . ."

"Okay, okay, supposing it's a total of $10,000. Is that possible? Can you give $5000 to each child?"

They looked at each other. "Tell you the truth," Mark said, "I'm not sure. Perhaps we could, but I have the feeling that would be a little tight."

"Okay. Don't worry about the exact amount right now," I told them. "We can figure out what you can comfortably afford later, after I ask you some questions and get a better idea of your whole financial situation. But for now let's say you'll give $5000 to each kid. I know we can actually work out a plan for less each year, but let me show you the general principle."

They both nodded and seemed to relax a bit.

"Let's suppose we put the money into an aggressive-growth mutual fund and it earns us 20% a year. Averages 20% a year over nine years, good ones and bad." I grabbed the calculator again and punched out 1.20 for the 20% a year, times 5000 for the first year's gift to Mark Junior, hit the equal sign nine times. "By the time your son is ready to start college, that first $5000 has grown to $25,799."

"We need $80,000," Charlotte said.

"So far we're only talking about the first year's gift," I explained. "In the second year of the plan, you put another

$5000 into the fund. It'll have one less year of growth, but in eight years it'll become — " I punched that out in a moment " — $21,499. So from the gifts of the first two years alone, we're going to provide $47,298, more than half the total amount we need."

"So if we do that for the next four years," Charlotte said, "we've got it."

I nodded.

"That doesn't seem possible," she replied, smiling.

"Basically that's the way it's done, Mrs. Daley," I told her. "I've oversimplified a bit, and in the real world it's not as easy as the example I gave you. But that's it."

"Seems incredible, Mark," she said.

He nodded. "I like it. I have some questions, but I like it, Mr. Cohen," he said. "Let me ask you this: I don't want to seem too piggish, but do we get to deduct those $5000 gifts as well?"

"Nope," I answered. "You get to shift the income taxes down to the level of the kids, but you can't also save by deducting the gift from your own income."

"I still like it," he said. "But that 20% rate? Aren't you being a little optimistic there?"

"Yes and no," I answered. I could pick a fund for them with a record that should bring us 20%. I would have to monitor it closely, move the money about if the market was shifting. And we might hit two or three bad years at a time when the Daleys needed to start paying for college. The fund could be down, and even though it would still show substantial appreciation, it could be a bad time to sell. Maybe the Daleys would have to dip into other assets to pull together the full amount that Mark Junior needed. Or Mark Junior might get a job, possibly financial aid, a student loan, something to cover the gap. Whatever kind of plan I set up for them, I would hope and expect that it would cover all the intended expenses, and over the years, I'd work to see that happen. But in the end we're talking about investments for a stretch of time, and we simply cannot predict every event.

They asked about more conservative approaches, and I told them that we could put the gifts into bonds, for example, ones that would mature as we needed the money. Our return would be fixed, say 10% rather than the 20% that we assumed with the aggressive mutual fund, but it would be a certain return. Or we could mix things up. Possibly buy some treasuries with some of the gift money, put some into a mutual fund, shift that to some bonds after a few years.

There were no restrictions so far as the tax law was concerned, nor were there any investment rules carved in stone, except for the famous "prudent man" rule, which says you have to be sound and judicious when investing a minor's money. "I would have to use my good judgment," I told them. "And you would have to feel comfortable with the plan and the way I invest."

They said they understood the general principles and the risks and wanted to get specific. I pulled together enough information from them for at least an outline of their financial condition.

"Like I thought," Mark said, "$5000 a year for each kid, $10,000 total, is a bit tight for us."

Reviewing the numbers, I could argue it either way. But there was no need to strap them. "Let's see what happens if we go for $4000 a child," I said, "and invest fairly cautiously."

Charlotte nodded. "I'd feel better all around with that approach," she said.

I did my simple computing trick, this time calculating the return on $4000 a year that would bring us 10% a year. "You'd have to spread your gifts over a greater number of years," I told them. "But you could have a fund of better than $70,000 if you contributed $4000 a year for ten years."

"And you said we'd need better than $80,000," Charlotte

said. "So we'd have to make up the difference one way or another."

"Maybe you wouldn't have to," I told her. "We've got the $70,000 when Mark starts college. If we take some $20,000 out that first year, we still have $50,000 working for us. That's another $5000 income for the next year. So, yes, maybe you'll have to pull some money together, but it certainly isn't going to be all that wrenching. And remember, none of this is etched in stone. All kinds of things could happen during ten years. Supposing you have one windfall, a bonus, someone leaves you $10,000? You could wipe out the whole deficit."

"And this is all taking the conservative approach?" Charlotte asked.

"Very conservative," I told her.

"God, darling," she said to Mark, obviously happy and relieved. "We can afford that. I know we can."

"I certainly think you can right now, Mrs. Daley, from the figures you've given me. And you're probably going to be earning more over these years, which will make it that much easier for you."

"There really is a light at the end of this tunnel," she said, almost sighing.

Her relief and pleasure were wonderful to witness. It's something all parents feel when we go through this. There is probably no other area of financial planning that gives such deep satisfaction and psychological pleasure as the thought that "I have taken care of my children."

My whole experience with the Daleys was an especially happy one. I not only showed them how they could build their college funds rather painlessly, I restored their faith in financial planning. The clincher evolved as I was reviewing their financial lives, trying to set up the best specific plans for their children. It turned out that Mark had what we call an "appreciated asset."

He was not a big or regular investor, but he was holding

one hundred shares of an electronics company, bought on a tip, naturally. Only this tip paid off. The stock had jumped from 10 to almost 30 in the eight months he had owned it, and he told me that his tipster was warning him he'd better sell.

Normally if he did that, he'd have a profit of $2000, but he'd have to pay the maximum tax on it, having held the stock for less than a year and a day. On his short-term gain, in his 42% bracket, he'd pay at least $840 to the IRS.

Again, gifting to the rescue. I explained to him that the law allowed us to take that stock and give it to one of the children. For tax purposes, the child would be getting a gift of one hundred shares of stock worth $30 a share. There would be no gift tax on that $3000 worth of stock, since, of course, the Daleys could give up to $20,000 without tax. The short-term tax that Mark Senior was facing on his $2000 profit would be wiped out for him. All that existed now was $3000 worth of the stock, sitting in his child's fund.

"But I still think we should sell that stock," Mark said. "Whether I own it or it's sitting in my son's account, that thing is certain to drop. If we don't take the profit now, we're going to lose everything."

"You can sell the stock the day you make the gift," I explained. "If you give it on Monday morning and it's selling at 30, and you sell it Monday afternoon for 30, there'll be a short-term tax on the $2000 gain, but at your child's tax rate. It'll be minuscule."

"So I can make a gift to Mark Junior of $3000 and save myself $840 in taxes as well?"

"You got it."

About a month after that meeting, I got a call from Mark. He and Charlotte had been thinking. They'd like me to do a full financial plan for them.

The same techniques may be applied to appreciated assets of various kinds.

I had a client with a piece of country real estate that had gone up in value about four times since he and his wife had bought it six years before. When they bought the five acres for $10,000, they weren't sure what they'd do with it, but they were sure land in that area was going to get expensive. And they were right. The whole area was now being "discovered" and a local appraiser told them their site was worth $40,000.

On my advice they made a gift of the property to their younger daughter, actually spreading the gift over two years. The first year they gave her a half interest in the land, which covered their $20,000 allowance for that year, and they gave her the other half the following year.

Just as we saw with Daley's gift of stock, the appreciated value of the land, $30,000, went tax-free for the parents. So far as the IRS was concerned, the property simply belonged to the child with a "basis," or cost, of $10,000. Whenever the land is sold to pay for the child's education or other needs, the taxes will be levied on the amount of profit between $10,000 and the selling price, and figured at the child's level.

Before making this move, we considered the tax effect if my clients kept the property themselves and made some other kind of gift to their daughter. After all, if they did sell the land themselves, they would pay only long-term gain rates, which for them would be 20% of their profit. We figured the child, however, would pay about 5% or 6%.

Another client owned a rental property, and we made gifts of it, at $20,000 a year, to a son. The income from the apartment building flowed directly to the child's custodial fund, with taxes, again, on the child's limited earnings only.

A Clifford trust is something of a variation on this use of an asset, with a major difference: You retain ownership of the asset.

If we wanted to use a Clifford trust with that apartment building, my client would put the building into the trust for ten years and one day, during which time the rental income would flow to the trust and the son would pay taxes at his low level. After the ten-year period, the ownership of the building would revert to my client.

The tax law limits the total amount you may put in a Clifford trust to about $45,000. Before you were allowed to make gifts up to $20,000 a year, the Clifford was one way around the lower gift limits (formerly as low as $3000). It has less value than it used to, but is still an appealing vehicle for parents who want to transfer income but retain principal.

A Crown loan is another device. Here you lend money to your child in the form of an interest-free demand loan. In theory you may demand payment at any time. In the meanwhile the money is invested and your child pays tax on the income and profits. The principal of shifting taxes operates again.

The problem with this one is that the IRS is continually challenging it. They say you have to pay them gift taxes on the loan. Until recently, they went to court over and over on this and always lost. Then they won a decision, which is presently being appealed. Most tax lawyers would, I think, tell you to take the chance if you want to set up a Crown loan. But if you are thinking of it, be sure to check with your own attorney.

Although both the Clifford trust and the Crown loan are techniques to consider, I would recommend them only if the basic custodial-fund approach is insufficient. If you want to go above the $20,000-per-couple level or if you want to get the asset back, then talk to your lawyer about them. Otherwise, set up custodial accounts and manage them as wisely as you can.

Checklist for Chapter 15

1. The law allows you to make a gift to anyone of up to $10,000 (up to $20,000 with your spouse), and there is no

gift tax on it. You may not deduct the amount of that gift from your taxes, but the income that the gift generates will belong to the person receiving the gift, and he will pay taxes at his level. This gifting, often used between parents and their children, allows the parents to transfer income from their own high tax brackets to their children, who normally start out with zero taxes. The tax on the income earned from the gifts, then, will be very, very low.

2. The gift is put into a custodial account of whatever sort of investment you, the parent, want. As the custodian, you decide how to invest the money — a bank account, a stock market account, real estate, whatever you think will best serve the child's needs.

3. Frequently such gifting and funds are established to cover future college expenses. Those amounts can be generally estimated and your investing plan worked out accordingly.

4. The gifts are irrevocable. You may not take them back or use them for any other purpose than the child's needs, although those needs may vary from time to time.

5. Once the child becomes a legal adult, and that age varies from state to state, all of the money in the fund is his to do with as he pleases. If that use is against the parent's wishes or the original intention of the gifts and the fund, there is little the parents can do.

6. Gifts need not be cash. Real estate, stocks, bonds and other assets may be gifted, and gifting appreciated assets is often a good strategy.

planning for retirement

IN COMMERCIALS, retirement is projected in association with a number of images: sun, golf, fishing, tennis, a handsome, trim, gray-haired couple strolling hand in hand down an empty beach.

In the real world, the images grow blurred for most people because retirement is extremely difficult for them to grasp in a concrete way. To begin with, it's a distant state, what seems an eternity away. And many of the people I meet can't really imagine themselves not working.

Still, it's a haunting matter. Especially at a time when "early retirement" is an increasingly common alternative in business.

So when people come to me for a financial plan and we talk about retirement, I frequently encounter a mix of vagueness and yearning. Young people excluded, since they can't accept any concept of retirement, never mind diverting their funds for such an incredibly distant time, the rest speak uncertainly of plans, but want me nonetheless to figure out just how much money they'll need to live "comfortably" — the common amorphous description — and how we can invest to achieve that.

The truth of the matter is that neither I nor any other planner can give them exact numbers. As when we planned for college educations for the Daleys' children, here we're also coping with too many variables. Still, we can and do plan.

I know there are planners who play the computer game with retirement, and I had a client practically walk out when I told her I couldn't do that for her. She was forty-two, divorced, certainly at a good point in life to start thinking about retirement. She had a friend who had gone to a planner I knew, and that woman had figured everything to the dollar.

I shrugged. "Okay, let me ask you some questions," I said, deciding on the most diplomatic way of making my point. "When do you intend to retire?"

"When?"

"Right. What age?"

Now *she* shrugged. "Sixty-five, I suppose."

"Okay, in twenty-three years. Where?"

"Where?"

"Well, the style you expect to live in, where you'll be living — these things affect what your new life style will cost you."

She thought a moment. "I'm not absolutely sure."

"You told me you are now earning $60,000 a year and you have an investment portfolio also worth about $60,000."

"Right."

"How much more do you expect to be earning and how much do you expect that portfolio to increase in twenty-three years?"

She stared at me. "That's ridiculous," she said. "How can I possibly estimate something like that?"

"You can't," I replied. "It is ridiculous. So is the whole idea of giving you an exact amount you're going to need the day after you turn sixty-five."

"Okay, okay, I got the message," she said. "But does that mean we can't have a retirement plan? I can't accept that."

"It doesn't mean that at all. We can have a plan, based on a number of intelligent principles."

First, I told her, at this stage in her life she should think of trying to maximize her net worth rather than aiming for a specific dollar amount for retirement.

As she got much closer to actual retirement, we could quantify and refine. But for now we could only gauge broadly. We could see what it costs her to live today. We could assume that unless she intends to become a permanent resident of the *Queen Elizabeth* and cruise the world first-class until she dies, her cost of living should diminish. She will eliminate, for example, all of her current expenses connected to business. Everything from clothes to commuting to lunches.

When she made a decision about where she was going to live in retirement, we could factor in the market value of her present home against the cost of the condo she would be buying in Sarasota, Santa Fe or wherever.

Our present state of uncertainty, however, did not mean we were helpless. On the contrary.

"My wife and I together," I told her, "have nine retirement plans. How many do you have?"

"You have nine?" she said, expressing the surprise I commonly encounter with this information. "Doesn't seem possible. I have a plan with my company and an IRA."

I spelled out my own. As an employee of a corporation, I have a deferred-compensation plan. Then I have an IRA and I also have a Keogh, which I fund with earnings from work outside the corporation as a consultant, writer, adviser. Last and least, I have Social Security.

My wife had been an official of the state of New York, and although she is no longer working with the state, she has a state pension plan. Today she is a psychotherapist, and from her private practice she maintains a Keogh. She teaches at a university and from that has a TSA plan, common to most nonprofit institutions. She has her own IRA and her own Social Security.

I stressed a point we saw illustrated earlier in the book: You've got to have as many retirement plans as possible.

They are the first step in any financial plan, not only because they are a way to provide for yourself in the future, but because they offer you a tax deduction today and a way to defer taxes until the time you're earning less so that your taxes on the money when you finally tap it will be less. That's a quinella. And the tax law gives it to you.

When you put that $2000 into an IRA (the maximum annual contribution for an individual), you are allowed to take a $2000 deduction from your earnings. With a Keogh plan, which in 1984 allows you to invest up to $30,000 a year, or 20% of your taxable earnings, you may deduct whatever you put into it. That much less tax you will pay this year, that much more you have working in your retirement fund. (We'll consider the elements of these and other retirement instruments later in the chapter.)

Investing philosophy

"I don't want to gamble with my retirement fund." In one form or another, I hear that over and over. People fearful that anything less than triple-A bonds will leave them penniless in their old age.

In fact, people who do that can cost themselves hundreds of thousands of dollars. Normally we are dealing with investments over so many years that the difference between compounding your money at 7% or 3% higher or lower can amount to a substantial sum.

Certainly with younger clients, I look for fairly aggressive investments to maximize our retirement pot. But young or old, I consider these retirement-fund investments in the context of the whole financial plan.

I had a case recently in which a man owned some tax-exempt bonds and an annuity. Those were his investments, and he paid no taxes on either, the bonds bearing no taxes, the annuity deferring taxes until he started drawing money from it.

He was an independent business consultant earning between $100,000 and $125,000 a year, depending on his volume, and was eligible for a Keogh plan. We set it up, taking the maximum we then could — 15% of his taxable income — and the first year that amounted to about $10,000. We bought common stocks with it. My plan was to produce as much growth as possible with those stocks. There wasn't a single blue chip among them.

The result was a balanced portfolio, even though the balance came from two different compartments that couldn't be merged.

In his own name he had the tax-free bonds and the annuity, producing interest. In the Keogh he had common stocks, which I could buy and sell without regard to how long I held them because even if I took short-term gains on the stocks, which normally for him would be whittled in half by taxes, in this case it didn't matter. The law says that there is no tax on anything in the Keogh and won't be until years from now when you tap those funds.

Now, if we had instead adopted the widespread and mistaken attitude of safety first with retirement funds, we would have reversed the plan. We would have put the common stocks in a regular trading account, one that had nothing to do with retirement plans. And with his Keogh money, we would have gone for the security of bonds and an annuity.

The effect would have been to punish the man doubly with taxes. All of his earnings on the stocks would be subject to taxes of one sort or another, short-term or long-term. And the tax benefits of his tax-free bonds and the annuity would be wasted. Since the Keogh plan shelters everything from current taxation anyway, we would be duplicating, or wasting, the law's protection. We would be putting investments that already are tax-free and tax-deferred into a plan that makes them tax-free and tax-deferred. A complete waste of the tax benefits.

Corporate retirement plans

Take whatever they give you.

If your company offers you a plan in which you contribute money from your salary and they contribute money from their treasury, there isn't any decision. You take it.

The only matter of choice is which sort of investment plan you want the company to put your program into. Often you'll have three or four options. They'll set your plan up with an aggressive-growth mutual fund; or some kind of fixed-income investment, such as a bond trust; or a money market fund; or a system to buy the company's stock.

I'm wary of buying the company's stock for your retirement plan. First, you have to make a judgment on your company's stock, analyze it as dispassionately as you would any other stock. It might be your company and you might have all kinds of wonderful feelings for the place, but if the market disagrees with you, you're going to be hurt.

Even if the company and the stock are strong, I have reservations. You're putting yourself in a risky position, collecting your salary from the company and investing your retirement fund with them as well.

About the only time I feel differently is when your company is not only a strong growth company, but they offer you the stock at a special discounted price. Then it can be tough to turn the offer down, especially when you can shift to one of the other alternatives after a while if you grow a bit less bullish on your company.

As for the other choices, your selection should be made in relation to other investments you're holding. If everything else is common stocks, you should balance that off with the bond plan.

A younger person would probably be wisest going for the growth stock plan, attempting to maximize his fund over the years.

Normally you can shift your plan from one alternative to another, with certain administrative time constraints. Companies don't want to be bothered moving your money around every Tuesday. Some allow quarterly switches, but many limit you to perhaps one change a year, often at a specific time of year. This can make life tough if your money is in the aggressive fund and the market starts to dive. You want to get out of that mutual fund and into the safety of a money market fund, but there's nothing you can do.

I've heard the argument that because of that, the smartest thing to do with a set of options such as I've described is to go into bonds and be done with it. Take the conservative route with this money and be aggressive with your own money in the market, where you and your broker can move as quickly as your best judgment tells you to.

I've also heard people who have placed their retirement plans in aggressive funds simply dismiss the time bind. Over the long haul, they maintain, they'll do well, better than the market as a whole. And, they add, there are plenty of people in the market with no restrictions on their movements at all, and they lose their shirts. Just because you are able to move out of the market, what guarantee is there that you'll know enough to do it?

It's a tough decision. I would favor the aggressive fund if that's appropriate to start with. Then each year, as the time approaches to inform the company of your choice for the coming year, make the best judgment you can. If you are worried, move into the money market fund.

Deferred compensation

A plan in which you defer compensation is not a "qualified" retirement plan. It is not subject to the many government regulations and protections of "qualified" plans, but it can be useful as part of your retirement strategy.

Essentially, this is a special arrangement you make with your employer. Unlike the regular plans, deferred compensation arrangements are not available to every employee. Rather, the employer decides which officers and key employees he'll extend this to.

It can be used to cut down your current taxes. I had a couple who were jointly earning about $125,000. His salary was $100,000 as an officer in a computer software company, and she brought home $25,000 working with a landscape architect. They had no children and did not plan to have any. When I looked over their sheet of living expenses, it was clear they could live on less income.

He went to the president of his company and got into a deferred comp plan. The company would now pay him at the rate of $80,000 a year, and they'd put $20,000 into the plan. Some companies invest the money or put it into high interest savings and money market accounts. My client's company simply did it through bookkeeping. They credited the account with the $20,000 a year, plus paid 10%-a-year interest. Once a month he received a statement from them.

All of the deferred salary and the interest would go to him when he retired from the company or, if he left sooner, on the day he walked out the door.

Fortunately, his company offered us options for withdrawing money on retirement. We were able to spread out the payments over a period of years, which would cut our taxes nicely.

The simple letter of agreement between my client and the company also stated that if he died, all the money due him would go to his wife.

So far as the tax law is concerned, the whole business was a nonevent. There would be no taxes on that deferred $20,-000 a year until my client took it out. Then he would have to pay taxes on the entire amount received, and pay at the full ordinary income rate.

Looming taxes on deferred income can frighten a person enough to keep him from leaving a company. Remember, if you leave before retirement, you have no choice. You may not elect to receive the accumulated loot over a period of years. You must take it all at once, and that can mean an awesome tax slug.

I have heard of cases where people turned down job offers because they figured out what that move would cost them in taxes on their deferred income and they decided the new job wasn't worth it.

With my client, about two and a half years after we set up the plan, he did receive a terrific offer from a competitor. By that time he had roughly $65,000 in the deferred comp plan, and a check for that amount would be handed him the day he left.

So I had him ask his new employers for help. They agreed and we set up a new plan. His new salary was to be $150,000. And the new company said they would allow him to defer $75,000 his first year, actually his first six months with them. That's all he had left on the calendar year. With such a large deferral, we were able to even things out. He had to take the $65,000 on the day he left his old company, but he deferred an equal amount of salary over the balance of the year from his new place, plus another $10,000 for his new deferred comp plan. His income for the year, in other words, did not rise for tax purposes.

What we did was perfectly legal, and we could only do it because we had a cooperative company and half a year to work with. If my client had shifted jobs in November, we would have been out of luck. There was never going to be enough income from the month of December alone to offset that big check.

One risk with deferred comp plans that you don't encounter with "qualified," government regulated retirement programs: Your company can go bankrupt and your deferred income sink with it.

With the qualified plan, your retirement money is set apart from the company's other assets. So no matter what happens to the company, you receive your money if the plan is funded.

With deferred comp, if there is a bankruptcy, you stand in line with the banks, the phone company, the stationery suppliers and everybody else to collect whatever you can of your own money.

Keoghs

This is the basic retirement plan for people who work for themselves and businesses that are not incorporated. You must be one or the other to benefit, and if you do, changes in the tax law allow you to benefit handsomely. Starting with 1984, you may put 20% of your taxable earnings — the amount after your deductions — up to $30,000 a year into a "defined contribution" Keogh. And every penny is deducted from your taxes.

By expanding the amount you're allowed to contribute up to $30,000 (there used to be a $7500 ceiling), Keoghs now make a lot of people hesitate before they incorporate.

Retirement plans alone were often sufficient reason to incorporate. Highly paid performers, doctors and other professionals were able to place huge amounts of their earnings into their own corporate retirement plans, money that otherwise would have been exposed to taxes.

By 1984, corporate plans and Keoghs will be pretty equal in terms of the size of the contribution you can make to them.

One important consideration for anyone setting up Keoghs for their unincorporated businesses: Whatever you put in for yourself, your company must contribute for your full-time employees. If you put 15% of your own earnings into your own Keogh, the company must contribute 15% of what your employee earns into his or her own Keogh. (One exception to this: Under some circumstances, high-earning employers can contribute as little as 7.5% to employees.) Keoghs used to be 100% "vested" from their first day, which meant that from the day you put money in for an employee, he was entitled to all of it. The new rules, applicable in 1984, allow vesting schedules that determine the percentage of contributions an employee gets according to his years of service.

You don't have to be earning big bucks to benefit from a Keogh. I had a client who sold his company, walked away with almost $2 million and retired at sixty-two. After one year he was going crazy from sitting around, so he started consulting.

Max earned between $20,000 and $25,000 a year as a consultant, an amount that seemed so small to him that he was genuinely surprised when I suggested we set up a Keogh for him and that income.

"This isn't a business, Stanley," he said. "It's therapy."

"You're still entitled to a Keogh. You're crazy not to take advantage of it. Why give the government money you don't have to?"

We set it up as an account with my brokerage house so that we could invest in common stocks. He put an average of $3000 a year into it, which of course he also deducted from his net income. As with other retirement plans, our earnings were not taxed or touched, but allowed to grow in the fund.

After five years the Keogh had grown to $43,000 and it is still growing. Max doesn't need the money, so we're planning to keep it in the Keogh until he is 70½, when the law requires him to start taking money out, even if only a small amount.

If we take it out as a lump sum, we'll take advantage of a special tax benefit: ten-year forward averaging. This allows you to calculate the taxes as if you were splitting up the total amount in the Keogh fund and taking it in ten yearly installments, even though you're actually taking it out in a lump sum. In Max's case, if he has $100,000 in the fund, we'll calculate as if he were going to receive $10,000 a year for ten years. We'll look at the tax table, see what the tax is for $10,000 of income for a single person — no matter what your actual status, that's the figure you use — and multiply that by ten. Max would have to make an upward adjustment to cover the minimum tax, but basically that's what he would have to pay on $100,000, a great deal less than if he paid at his regular level.

As noted, we put Max's yearly Keogh investments into the market, and the choices of where you may put your own Keogh are broad — a bank, a mutual fund, an insurance company, a brokerage firm. And a new provision allows you to be your own custodian if you want. I don't like banks for Keoghs because they don't offer you a wide enough range of investments.

Whichever form you choose, you're free to change. If you start with a bank and decide you can do better with a mutual fund, you simply transfer your account. There's no tax or penalty from the IRS. Some institutions, banks especially, will hit you with a penalty if you transfer your funds out of a time deposit before the time is up. But that is between the bank and you. It is not part of the law on Keoghs.

There are some restrictions on investments with Keoghs: no margin accounts, no short positions on stocks, and a list of "hard assets" you may not invest in, diamonds, gold and paintings among them.

One aspect of this plan commonly overlooked is the "voluntary." It is a way of putting more money into your Keogh. Under present rules in 1984, voluntaries have been liberalized. There used to be a $2500 ceiling on these, and you could only have one in a plan that included employees. Now anyone can do a voluntary with up to 10% of his income.

You may not take this extra "voluntary" amount and deduct it from your taxes, as you would with the regular contribution. But you may have the extra money work as part of the fund, with the earnings tax-deferred over the years until you take money out. And it is that tax deferral, that extra chance to have money compounding without current taxation, that makes this device so worthwhile. I almost always recommend it.

Another possibility with the Keogh is the defined-benefit plan. It permits a contribution of even larger amounts, but it has complications. Very high income people might want to discuss this with a planner or a pension actuary.

IRAs

By now these must be America's most famous retirement plans. They are simple and, so far as I'm concerned, mandatory. I insist with all my clients, no matter how wealthy, that they maintain IRAs.

These used to be available only to people who didn't have retirement plans where they worked. But now everyone can have them, no matter how many other retirement programs you maintain.

The maximum yearly contribution is $2000, and all you have to do to put that much in is to earn $2000. If you earn less, you can invest an amount equal to everything you earn.

Like the Keogh investments, whatever you put into an IRA is tax deductible, and all of your investments and earnings are tax-deferred until you pull the money out. You may start to draw that money at 59½, and you *must* start to draw it out by 70½.

When you take it out, it's all considered "ordinary income" and so taxed at your highest rate. And you do not have the option of ten-year-forward tax-averaging that you have in the Keogh. You have five-year averaging available to you at any time, of course. (Whenever you have a year in which your income is significantly higher than you showed in each of the four preceding years, you may average out those five years so you don't get walloped so badly for that extraordinary year.)

If you withdraw IRA or Keogh money before age 59½, you face penalties from the IRS, as well as taxes.

Like Keogh, the range of IRA investment possibilities is great, and once again, I think the worst place is a bank.

With the new law permitting everyone to have IRAs, the number of my clients starting them has mushroomed. In the early years, obviously, their funds are not going to amount to very much, and at this level I recommend a mutual fund in the Oppenheimer Group of funds. They have some aggressive growth funds with tremendous records. For clients who have maintained IRAs for a number of years and who have amounts in them we can do something with, I usually put their money into the stock market.

One thing that's deceptive about IRAs is in fact their growth potential. It's true you start small, and these days especially, people tend to think that $2000 is so little. But they overlook the effect of compounding.

If you had put $2000 a year with the Oppenheimer Special Fund from 1973 through 1982, or a $20,000 total investment, your fund would have risen to $87,450. There is no guarantee that another ten-year period would work out as well, of course, yet you can see what's possible with small annual contributions.

Rather than demeaning the IRA by dismissing the $2000

contribution as paltry, I show my clients the arithmetic and then push them to put their money in during the first week of January. Give yourself as much time each year as possible to have that tax-deferred money working for you, I tell them.

When it comes time to take the money out

A few additional notes on pulling money out of IRAs and Keoghs.

You do not have to take all the money out at once. When you hit 70½, you must begin to draw from the fund, if you haven't started already. You may start at 59½.

But if you find that you really don't need that additional income from the IRA or the Keogh and would prefer to see it work for you, there is a formula that determines how little you may take out. Basically it divides the amount in the fund by the number of years on your life-expectancy chart. If the chart says you've got fifteen years to go, you must draw out one-fifteenth in the first year, one-fourteenth the next year, one-thirteenth the year after and so on. (If you have a spouse, you may use the combined life expectancies of the two of you, which will further reduce the amount you must withdraw.)

With IRAs, when you hit 70½ you must begin the withdrawal process and you must also stop contributing to them. Keoghs are different. You may contribute to them, as long as you are employed and have earned income, until you die.

I've had many clients who continued working until their late 70s. And every year we socked another 15% of their earnings back into the Keogh. At the same time they had to take a minimal amount out of the fund, having passed 70½.

In most of these cases, the people never needed the fund for their living expenses, so when they died, their wonderfully blooming Keoghs went to their estates and their heirs.

Using the IRA rollover. We spoke earlier in the chapter of deferred compensation and the trickiness of handling your accumulated funds if you leave your company to take another job. Your old boss hands you a check for tens of thousands of dollars, and unless you're smart and fortunate, you're going to pay a substantial amount of extra taxes that year.

If, however, you have a pension plan at a corporation and you leave, you have a simple alternative that will spare you taxes. You may do an "IRA rollover."

You deposit the funds from your former retirement plan into an IRA rollover. There are no penalties, taxes, nothing. You have simply converted from one kind of retirement program to another. If you choose a partial rollover, which used to be prohibited but is now allowed, you pay tax only on the money you don't roll over but take out of the pension plan.

If you are going from a state of self-employment to a job with a corporation, from a Keogh to a corporate plan, you have another matter.

Do nothing with the Keogh. While working for the corporation, you will not be allowed to make additional contributions to the Keogh plan, but it will continue to earn money as always.

One confused man came to me, having made a disastrous mistake with his Keogh. He had a small management-consulting firm, and as often happens in that work, he did such a good job for one company, they hired him to run the place.

At the time he had about $350,000 in his Keogh plan. He took it out and put it into an IRA rollover. By doing so, he lost the ten-year forward-averaging on taxes. IRAs don't have that benefit. If he had left the Keogh alone, he would have had a "frozen Keogh." He could not make any more contributions to it so long as he worked for a corporation, but he could manage the money in that fund, enjoy tax-deferred growth just as before and save himself lots of tax dollars when he finally took the money by applying ten-year averaging.

Annuities

Phil and Marian Doremus were two extremely conservative people. They had $30,000 in the bank, they told me in their first visit with me; what they liked about it was that the $30,000 was absolutely safe, and they were earning 8% interest on it.

I went into my litany. That 8% interest meant 4% for Uncle Sam and 4% for Mr. and Mrs. Doremus after taxes. And with the inflation rate at 6%, that nice safe bank account was losing them 2% a year.

They could certainly understand the math, but emotionally their hearts were still in that bank vault. They wanted an investment for retirement that would make them some real money, they told me, and yet be entirely safe.

I did have one that met all of their requirements, one that I use frequently for other, less conservative people as well.

It is a "single-premium deferred annuity," or SPDA. "Single premium" because you buy it with one lump-sum payment; there are no annual premiums to pay. "Deferred annuity" because you take your annuity payments sometime after you put the money in, usually many years later.

We bought a $30,000 SPDA in Marian's name, with Phil as beneficiary. The insurance company that sold it to us specified that we would get an interest rate of 11%, guaranteed for one year.

The Doremuses had been getting 8% from the bank, and the money had disappeared. Either they spent it or it went in taxes. Although I didn't know what interest they would receive on their annuity after the first year, I could still make a projection that dazzled them. I assumed that from the second year on, they would get only 8%, the same as their bank rate — a much lower figure than I really believed they'd be getting. I tapped out the figures on my trusty hand-held calculator.

After one year at 11% their annuity would have a value of $33,000. After five years at 8% it would be worth $44,896, and after twenty years, $142,418. When the Doremuses are sixty-two years old, their money will have more than quadrupled.

Annuities can be either "load" or "no-load." I use only no-load annuities, which means that every penny of the Doremuses' $30,000 was earning interest from the day it was invested. There is a catch to no-load annuities. If the insurance companies don't get you going in, they'll get you going out; they charge a fee, or "back-end load," if and when you withdraw your money. So you want to avoid that back-end load — not too hard to do.

For one thing, most companies use a declining scale for these fees. Typically you'll pay 6% if you withdraw all of the money in the first year, 5% in the second year and so on down to zero charges in the sixth year. If you stay with the annuity for more than six years, then you never pay a fee. But more important, if at some future date you "annuitize the contract," that is to say, establish a schedule of monthly payments for a period of years or for life, you also pay no fee.

Phil and Marian Doremus were both forty-two years old, and both were working. We assumed, but were by no means sure, that they would both retire at age sixty-five. With the annuity, we didn't have to be sure of their future plans. For such a safe investment, free of "downside risk," an annuity is remarkably flexible. Most annuity contracts provide upward of a dozen payment options. You don't specify how you will be paid when you buy the annuity. All of the options are available for your use at any time, and you notify the company which payment plan you want at the time you wish to start receiving payments. Or you may ask for a lump-sum payment.

Until you make your decision, your money is compounding annually, without any current taxation, at whatever rate the insurance company agreed to pay you. The Doremuses had guaranteed safety of principal. There was no way that they could have less than their original $30,000. If they simply forgot about their annuity contract, the only thing that would happen to it would be the accumulation of additional money as their interest built up. That interest would not even be declared on their tax return.

Phil and Marian didn't know exactly what the value of their contract would be because the interest rate was specified for only the first year. But they did have a particular rate safeguard. When they took out their SPDA, the company not only specified a one-year rate of 11%, it also specified a "lower limit" of 10%. The company would notify them in advance of each contract anniversary what the next year's rate would be, and if that rate fell below the lower limit of 10%, the Doremuses could transfer their annuity to another company without paying the back-end load. Of course, once the load charges had expired after six years, they could transfer without charge regardless of what the rate might be.

This had the effect of keeping Marian Doremus's insurance company competitive: It had to pay her a rate of 10% or more, or risk losing her. That's why I doubted that the rate would ever drop as low as the 8% I used for my projections. (Nowadays there are some companies that give five-year rate guarantees. This is very attractive, although the rates are usually slightly lower than one-year guarantees and the back-end load often stays at the top level for all five years.)

In considering how and when to withdraw money, the Doremuses will have to be alert to the IRS rules that govern annuities. The law says that if you withdraw a lump sum of money prior to age 59½ or before you have owned an annuity for ten years, a penalty of 5% of the amount withdrawn is charged.

Also, whatever you withdraw is subject to taxation on the

interest portion, but not on the part that is principal. Let's say that the Doremuses decide to take a lump sum out of their annuity to buy a house. More than ten years have gone by and their $30,000 annuity is now worth $67,000. If they withdraw $37,000, all of that amount is taxable at ordinary income rates, but since more than ten years have passed, there is no penalty. If they withdraw $40,000, they still pay tax on only $37,000 because the additional $3000 they are taking out is part of their original principal.

For the Doremuses, a more likely possibility is to annuitize, to take periodic payments rather than a lump sum. If they do retire at the age of sixty-five, at that time Marian might opt for annuity payments for "life with ten years certain." She would receive about $1,795 each month for the rest of her life. If she died before the expiration of ten years, Phil would receive the same payments for the balance of the ten years. A fraction of these payments would be tax-free.

Marian could also have chosen a life income with no guaranteed "years certain," or life with fifteen years certain, or a joint and survivor annuity, or an annuity for a definite number of years — five years or ten years or whatever. The insurance company figures out actuarially what each option ought to pay, and they will notify Marian Doremus of the figure before she commits herself.

I had a very different use for an annuity with Olivia Dobbs. She was thirty-nine and had recently been widowed. Her husband, Richard Dobbs, an optometrist, died of a heart attack at fifty-seven. He left Olivia with two boys, aged thirteen and twelve, and a fairly substantial estate.

We set about to invest that estate money quite conservatively. Olivia had been a housewife, and since she had very little working experience and two children to support, we couldn't afford to take chances. She did expect to get a job eventually, but she felt that the loss of their father was enough of a blow to the two boys. She wanted to stay home with them until they reached college age.

When Olivia would start earning a salary, in about five years, she would have enough money to live on. And the investments that we were setting up would provide growth and assets to pay for college for both her sons. Our problem was that we didn't have enough current income for the five years until the boys started college and she got a job. We figured we needed $9000 a year to fill the gap. An annuity solved that problem.

We took $100,000 from Olivia's estate money and told the insurance company that we wanted an immediate annuity for five years, which would produce $750 per month or $9000 a year.

The insurance company figured out how much money would have to be applied to fund the payments of $9000 a year. It came to about $39,000.

The balance of our $100,000, or $61,000, went into a second, deferred annuity with an 11% rate, guaranteed for five years. After five years the immediate annuity would come to an end, and the $61,000 compounded at 11% would have grown to $102,700.

So Olivia would have $9000 a year to live on, and at the end of five years she would end up with more money than she started with. Again, we don't have to decide what we'll do in the future. At the end of the five years, Olivia could leave the $102,700 in the annuity to compound itself up to perhaps $150,000 or $160,000 over the next five years. The point is options and flexibility.

There are some fortunate people who have annuities taken out prior to August 14, 1982, and those people have some special privileges that are not currently available. You can borrow against old annuities, pay interest on the loan, deduct the interest charges from your taxes and at the same time have the annuity continue to compound itself without any tax. All this is done by simply presenting the annuity at the bank and using it as collateral.

On these old annuities, you can also draw money out in lump-sum amounts without taxation, providing that the amount drawn does not exceed the amount you originally put in. Under the old law, the first money you withdraw is considered a return of your own capital and, therefore, not taxable. So a person with an old annuity that was taken out with a lump sum of $50,000 could draw up to $50,000 from that contract, and even if the contract were still worth $75,000, $100,000 or whatever, that $50,000 would be tax-free.

Most annuities, old and new, allow the withdrawal of up to 10% of the money in any given contract year, without any penalty charge from the insurance company. If you have an old-law annuity, you can take advantage of that. But with a new-law annuity, if you are less than 59½ years old and have had the annuity for less than ten years, a 10% withdrawal will cause you some problems with the IRS.

I am not overly disturbed by the new law. It is nice to be able to borrow against an annuity, and for a few people there is an advantage in being able to take out small lump sums. But the basic merit of an annuity is that it permits you to compound your money, with great safety, at a high rate for an extended period of time without current taxation and then to withdraw the money in the form of periodic payments that will help finance your retirement.

Single-premium whole life

Single-pay annuities do not provide life insurance. They provide a safe, painless way to guarantee income at retirement or some other period of your life, but there is no life insurance element in them.

In recent years, life insurance companies have also been

offering a single-premium whole life insurance policy, which resembles the annuities.

With single-pay life you cover all of your premiums with a lump sum, and the insurance company calculates a portion of your money for insurance and a portion for investment, just as they do if you buy a regular whole life policy and pay them premiums on a yearly basis. Only there is a difference.

With the single-premium policy, the investment aspect of your policy is emphasized over the insurance aspect. As a result, instead of being paid at the rate of, say, 5% that you'd receive from a whole life policy, you would see something on the order of maybe 10%. It would be slightly lower than what competing annuity plans are offering.

This 10% will increase your "cash-surrender value" or "loan value" of the policy in the same way that a portion of your annual premiums increases that value with regular whole life. And just as you may with whole life, with the single premium you may borrow against that increasing amount.

That is different from annuities. As noted, the present law does not allow you to borrow against them.

The loan feature was a part of the old annuity plan that in itself attracted some big operators. You could end up with a loan issued on the basis of the annuity's expanded value, and a pile of cash with no taxes attached was an enticing tax ploy.

Since the law no longer allows borrowing on new annuity programs, some people favor the single-premium life plan. There you have the same protection of your principal, but you also have access to a chunk of money if you need it.

In practice, I rarely see a sufficient need to touch the money in an annuity. And since annuities are at this writing (June 1983) still paying higher rates than insurance plans, I favor them for this kind of planning.

Checklist for Chapter 16

1. Until you are fairly close to actual retirement, you won't be able to project exact dollar amounts to cover all your future needs. Too many variables and unknowns. Your basic objective should be to maximize your net worth.

2. Have as many retirement plans as you possibly can. Not only will they provide you with funds tomorrow, they are tax deductions today.

3. Forget the cliché that you must invest conservatively when it comes to retirement plans. Invest in relation to all the rest of your investments and your particular financial profile. Aim for balance in the kinds of investments you maintain.

4. With corporate retirement plans, take whatever your company offers you. If they give you a choice of where to invest the funds, once again make your decision in relation to your other investments. In many cases I recommend the investment with the chance of the greatest growth.

5. If you work for a corporation and it offers a deferred comp plan, consider it as a way of deferring taxes and building your retirement income. But be prepared for what can be a very large lump-sum payment, and very substantial taxes on it, if you leave your company before retirement. You might use your new company and its deferred comp plan to spare you a crushing tax blow.

6. Keoghs are available to self-employed people and unincorporated businesses. By 1984, you will be allowed to put up to $30,000 into them, take your contribution as a deduction and defer taxes on it until you take the money out. Further, at that time you can take advantage of a ten-year tax-averaging plan to cut your taxes. You have several options for setting up your Keogh, from depositing it with a conservative bank to setting up an account with a stockbroker.

7. IRAs are a must for everyone. No matter how many other retirement plans you maintain, you may also have an

IRA. You may contribute up to $2000 a year and take a deduction for the amount. Like Keoghs and other retirement programs, all your contributions and earnings are tax-deferred until you tap the funds after age 59½. Don't be deceived by the relatively small amount allowed for your annual contribution. If you had deposited $2000 a year for the ten years from 1973 through 1982 in the Oppenheimer Special Fund and let your contributions and dividends compound, your fund would have grown to $87,450. In another period the gains will vary, but the principle of compounding won't.

8. When you draw money out of Keoghs and IRAs, you may choose a lump sum or spread the payments over the years. Also, if you don't need the money and want to leave it in to work further for you and your estate, there is a way to set up minimal payments only. But you must take something each year after you reach 70½.

9. An IRA rollover is useful if you are leaving a corporation and taking the money out of their retirement plan. Simply have the accumulated funds from the plan shifted to an IRA rollover, and you will keep the tax deferral. No taxes, penalties, nothing, merely a shift of plans. However, do not transfer your Keogh into an IRA rollover or you'll lose the ten-year tax-forwarding option. IRAs do not have that.

10. Single-premium annuities are useful for retirement planning, security and a variety of pay-out plans. They offer growth and all earnings are tax-deferred. And when you take money out of the annuity, you pay taxes on what your annuity has earned over the years.

11. Single-premium whole life insurance is like an annuity, offering an investment element, but it also gives you life insurance. You cover all the premiums with one payment, which then provides you insurance and an investment. The investment side of your policy will pay something less than a single-premium annuity, but you can borrow from the insurance policy, which you cannot do with an annuity.

CHAPTER 17

How to get good financial planning advice for yourself

WE'VE COVERED quite a bit of ground in this book, but the range in fact is no more than you should expect from anyone who does your financial planning.

A good planner is above all a generalist, familiar with the complete spread of techniques and instruments, with all of the areas your financial well-being requires.

And when I say "familiar," I mean more than just a glib delivery of vague outlines. The planner's knowledge should be broad, substantial and detailed. He has to know about everything from over-the-counter stocks to trusts and estates to mortgages. If his knowledge and background amount to real competence with only one or two kinds of investments or one area of financial strategy, he can't possibly do a proper job for you.

You may need him to work with other professionals. If you have an established relationship with an accountant and a lawyer, you'll want to be sure your planner will fit well with them. His job will be to coordinate everybody's efforts, and to do that he's got to be able to talk the same language as the lawyer and the accountant, and maintain their respect.

Sometimes a good place to begin your search for a planner is in fact with your accountant and lawyer. They are familiar with your financial life, more than you are. What planners can they recommend? Have they sent other clients with similar conditions and problems as yours to certain planners?

In your search, talk to friends and colleagues earning more or less what you do. Their requirements will be close to yours, and if they've found a planner they can recommend, ask them the basic questions: How does the man work? What is his approach in developing the plan? Does he only draw up a plan, or does he also implement it? Does he give you the time you need, make himself available on the phone when you've got a question? What does he charge? Does he explain things the way you want, in English and not financial jargon? What sort of experience does he have? Is he, in fact, a Certified Financial Planner? What sorts of clients does he have? What's his investment record been? Does he approach a client with a long-range view of things and expect a long-term relationship?

Bear in mind a few conditions of the trade. First, not all planners will accept all clients. You want someone who indeed does planning for people like yourself. But you might not show enough income to be accepted by some planners. In Los Angeles, for example, there are several "money managers" who specialize in the likes of Barbra Streisand. They won't talk to anyone who earns less than $300,000 a year. Elsewhere I've heard of minimums of $100,000 and I've heard of planners with no such rules. I am one of them.

Nearly all of my clients come to me as referrals from other, presumably satisfied customers. And some years ago I realized that even if someone was earning so little there wasn't much of a plan I or anyone could concoct for him, I couldn't turn him away; I'd be insulting the other well-meaning client who sent him to me.

There are some people earning, say, $25,000 or $30,000 who come to me, and all I can do is set them up with an IRA, maybe put a few dollars for them into a mutual fund. That's not a plan, but it is the beginning of something. We hope that the account and fund will grow and so will their careers. And then we can do some real planning.

You'll notice a sense of mutuality running through this: clients sending me their friends and colleagues because they like what I've been doing for them.

That's terribly important for you, the personal referral. It means that the planner you select has to produce for you and satisfy you, or not only won't you send him anyone else, but he will lose you as a client, and possibly the person who originally sent you as well. Believe me, I know how those links are formed. It's terribly important to me that they don't get broken.

That's one reason why you want to be careful about planners you only hear about, perhaps see on a TV show, but have no personal connection with. They might be okay, but on the other hand their real specialty might not be planning but personal public relations. If they don't do such a good job for you, no great loss. They simply get themselves on another TV show and attract new customers. I don't mean to sound arbitrary and absolute here, especially since I appear on some TV shows and do a certain amount of lecturing. But I think you can see my distinction and caution.

If you simply cannot find anyone who can recommend a planner to you, then write to the Institute of Certified Financial Planners, 3443 South Galena St., Suite 190, Denver, CO 80231, or the International Association for Financial Planning, 5775 Peachtree Dunwoody Rd., Suite 120C, Atlanta, GA 30342.

All of the members of the first organization, the Institute, are graduates of the College for Financial Planning in Denver. They'll send you a list of Certified Financial Planners in your area, with some information on their backgrounds.

This is not as good as having the personal connection, but at least you know you'll have people who are trained and certified. If you go this route, you ought to talk to three people from the names you've received before you make a choice.

So far as I'm concerned, the only certification that's worthwhile is the one from the College for Financial Planning. But having said that, I should add that the college was only started in 1972, and indeed the whole field of professional financial planning is very new. An old-timer is someone who began planning, perhaps, in the late 1960s. (The college's program, by the way, is two years of courses covering the basic subjects a planner should know. Some people take the courses by correspondence. Others study under some one hundred adjunct faculty members or at fifty affiliated colleges around the country.)

The International Association for Financial Planning is the trade association for the industry, with no formal college, although it does run an extensive program of seminars and meetings. Its members are not necessarily Certified Financial Planners.

IAFP is organizing a registry, as I write, to which they will be able to refer queries for financial-planning help.

In the flesh

Go have your interviews. Beyond any particular questions you might toss at a planner, there is quite a bit from this book you can use as litmus.

How does the planner go about investing in the stock market, for example? What sort of experience in that area does he have? Is he also a stockbroker, as I am, in addition to being a financial planner? If not, how does he execute orders? What kind of research is available to him?

I know of planners who don't invest in the market directly. They don't have the time or facilities, so they take the money that would otherwise go into the market and buy shares of mutual funds. Since mutual funds can be tracked, you can readily see how well they and the planners have done. As we've seen, I use mutual funds myself, but in my mind there is nothing like managing the portfolio yourself, assuming good management of course. What your potential planner thinks in this regard is extremely important and should be brought out in your exploratory session.

One area of inquiry I consider fruitless is generally called "philosophy." "What is your philosophy when it comes to investing?" people ask me, and I don't know what to answer, short of making a three-hour speech. Usually that question presumes a high degree of fear of risk. If you ask a potential planner about his investment philosophy, he will tell you exactly what he thinks you want to hear.

What about shelters? Does his firm offer them? How many and what kinds? Again, you want variety, flexibility. I know of planning firms that maintain contacts with only one or two shelter syndicators. What they are offering simply might not be best for you.

Independent financial-planning shops can be good, and often you can make a judgment on them as you would some other service in your community. How long have they been in business? What is their reputation? How large a staff and with what kind of training? What facilities do they maintain?

Part of your judgment in making your selection will be subjective. Do you feel comfortable with this person? When he answers a question about a specific concern, is he being specific? Or is he waffling, making a little speech that sounds like something he turns on for everybody who comes into his office?

Perhaps the most important matter to clarify is technique. Does he only devise the plan, or does he also implement it? And here there is a certain amount of debate as to which is better.

I have no doubts at all. It is far, far better to have the person who is creating the plan also carry it out. Otherwise you get an academic plan. Planning and implementation must be unified: Theory and practice go together.

If your planner says, "You need tax-free bonds," he's got to know which ones, and he's got to know yields and quality, and whether we should buy them at par or at a discount, and what's the condition of the tax-exempt bond market right now, today, when we're buying. If your plan is being devised by someone removed from the daily commerce of that market, he's not going to know.

I've seen plans that recommended tax shelters without any reference to what was available and appropriate or even what particular category of shelter the client needed.

Some of the larger brokerage firms have tried this fragmented system. Your broker in that firm puts you together with a planner in the firm. He spends two and a half hours interviewing you and filling out forms that he then runs through the firm's computer. Out comes 150 pages, and that's the end of your relationship with the planner.

If the printout says you should have a trust agreement, well, you go to your lawyer and tell him that apparently you should have one of these things, even though you aren't really sure what it is or why you need it.

If the plan says you should have $50,000 worth of tax-exempt bonds, presumably you are supposed to call the broker you started with and tell him: "According to page 86, it says $50,000 worth of tax-exempt bonds . . ." and presumably he'd go and buy them.

A good plan cannot be created that way. It has to be tailored to your particular financial shape and condition. And then brought to life by its designer.

Resolving the classic conflict

Against this is the argument that if the same person who designs your plan also implements it, how can he be dispassionate? How can you be sure that he'll put your interests first? How can you be sure that, for example, if the planner is also a stockbroker, he won't recommend that you buy thousands of dollars' worth of stocks so he can reap his sweet commissions? Or ditto, if he recommends a shelter, for which he'll receive a commission? Or insurance?

It is a problem, no question. In the real world, every profession tends to sell what it makes money on. Surgeons like to operate, lawyers like to litigate, brokers churn accounts.

But you are not defenseless.

First, there is that personal recommendation and the chain you become part of. Good business depends on continuing growth, not a few fat commissions.

When a planner is recommended, get a full reading of the success he's brought your friend and for how long a time. If your friend has two or three years of work with the planner, you've got a good record there to analyze. Also, if they have been together that long, presumably it's because the results have been good.

If you have some doubts, there is no law that says you must put an entire plan into effect immediately. You can always tell the planner, "Let's go ahead with your recommendations for, say, stocks and bonds right now, but I'd like to wait a bit on the rest." Try him out yourself for a while.

Continue to educate yourself. Throughout this book I've told you about my clients and how the best of them learn, keep up with the market, stay deeply involved in what we do with their money. I've shared with you the continuing debates and tugs-of-war I have with them. Do the same with your planner. He'll do a better job than if you're passive. And if he's not responsive or if he brushes you off, that's all you need to know. Get yourself another planner.

How much will it cost?

What you are charged will somewhat depend on how the planner works.

If he does only the plan, expect his fee for it to be higher than if he were also going to collect commissions for carrying it out.

I charge somewhere between $450 and $3500 to do a plan, depending on its complexity and size, the amount of computer services we need and the total assets to be managed. And I receive whatever the standard commissions and fees are for the investments I make.

I assume, and I tell anyone coming to me the first time, that we'll have a continuing relationship and I will carry out the plan. But no one must stay with me or with any planner. You may take the plan and wrap fish in it and decide not to follow a single step suggested.

Be clear about any charges along the way. Most planners don't charge any kind of maintenance fee.

Most importantly, be clear and certain that you may consult with your planner at any time, within reason.

The big planning departments of major brokerage firms will charge anywhere from $3000 to $7000 for a plan.

Planners, by the way, normally will not charge you for that first meeting when you're looking around.

Beware

In the last year or so, there have been various programs started by some large financial institutions, brokerage houses, banks and insurance companies to offer so-called financial-planning services.

I would be extremely wary of any employee of an insurance company who offered his talents as a financial planner. I would have to suspect that he had merely found yet another way to try and convince me to buy millions of bucks' worth of insurance that I don't really need.

I was a stockbroker before I also became a planner. If you can't find a certified planner you like, a broker might do the job if he really has the kind of breadth and depth we're looking for. Among other things, his brokerage house probably has all the investment vehicles that you'll need — stocks, bonds, unit trusts, tax shelters, options, annuities. Anyone whose shop is lacking some of the major kinds of investments is likely to offer you what *he* has, not what *you* ought to have.

But you'll have to make a sharp judgment on anyone who called you a few months ago to peddle a stock and is back on the phone now suggesting that you get together for an entire financial plan.

He may not pass scrutiny. But I would strongly recommend that you find someone to work with. Doing it all yourself is extremely difficult, if not impossible, especially for a part-time amateur. But an informed part-time amateur and a good professional planner make a splendid team.

One final thought: Handling your money, surviving on $50,000 to $150,000 a year, even prospering from it, is certainly possible, as I hope I've shown you in the course of this book. To do it right, as in doing so many things right, treat life like an open-book test. Keep coming back to this book when you've got questions and worries about your financial life, checking what I've said, and do the same with other books. Then, armed, thrash it about with your planner. It's a continuing process. That's how the two of you will produce, not miracles, but shiny solutions.

Index

ABOUT THE AUTHORS

Stanley J. Cohen is a Certified Financial Planner, formerly a director of the Institute of Certified Financial Planners and the founder of the Institute's *Journal*. A stock broker for almost twenty years, he is senior vice-president of the brokerage firm of Moseley, Hallgarten, Estabrook & Weeden, and former president of the New York Investment Round Table. He lives with his wife, Fimi, in New York.

Robert Wool is co-author of *All You Need to Know About the IRS*, and *All You Need to Know About Banks*. Formerly the political editor of *The New York Times Magazine*, editor in chief of *The Washington Post Magazine*, and executive editor of *New York* magazine, he is presently editor in chief of *Tax Angles*, the tax newsletter, and president of Premier Cru Books, Inc., his New York book packaging company. He lives with his wife, Bridget, and two daughters, Vanessa and Zoe, in New York.